How Music Changed YouTube

How Music Changed YouTube

Guillaume Heuguet

BLOOMSBURY ACADEMIC
NEW YORK · LONDON · OXFORD · NEW DELHI · SYDNEY

BLOOMSBURY ACADEMIC
Bloomsbury Publishing Inc
1385 Broadway, New York, NY 10018, USA
50 Bedford Square, London, WC1B 3DP, UK
29 Earlsfort Terrace, Dublin 2, Ireland

BLOOMSBURY, BLOOMSBURY ACADEMIC and the Diana logo are trademarks
of Bloomsbury Publishing Plc

First published in the United States of America 2024

© Institut national de l'audiovisuel, 2021
© Guillaume Heuguet, 2021, 2024

Cover design by Studio Auto

A catalog record for this book is available from the Library of Congress.

ISBN: HB: 979-8-7651-0071-4
           PB: 979-8-7651-0070-7
           ePDF: 979-8-7651-0073-8
           eBook: 979-8-7651-0072-1

Typeset by RefineCatch Limited, Bungay, Suffolk
Printed and bound in Great Britain

To find out more about our authors and books, visit www.bloomsbury.com
and sign up for our newsletters.

Contents

Acknowledgements

First, I am forever grateful for Clémence Polès, for reasons that go well beyond the scope and purpose of this book.

This book is based on questions that are first and foremost collective. I would like to thank the small equally-minded community of researchers, critics, publishers, musicians, enthusiasts and friends with whom I have had the pleasure of discussing the state of music, technology and media over many years, including all the Audimat contributors, as well as Etienne Menu, Agnès Gayraud, Olivier Lamm, Pierre Arnoux, Frank Rebillard, Will Straw, Philippe Le Guern, Gérôme Guibert, Jean-Samuel Beuscart, François Debruyne, Sophie Maisonneuve, Loic Riom, Stéphane Roth, John Seabrook, Alexandre Cortay, Paul Régimbeau, Charlie Janiaut, Maxime Barré, Thibault Proulx, Michael Spanu, Lorenzo Targhetta, François Ribac, and the IASPM-BFE.

Very special thanks goes to Sophie Garnier, who had a great hand in helping with the translation of this book. I could not have done it without her. And to Pauline Chasseray-Peraldi, whose support, reading and editing of the original thesis that led to this book were invaluable.

The support of my thesis supervisor Adeline Wrona was fundamental in me pursuing the research in the first place. Although not always made explicit in the book, her analysis of the relationship between media and literature has been an important inspiration.

I am also indebted to Joëlle Le Marec, as well as to the participants in the "Knowledge of music, studies of science" program and the Cultures of inquiry seminar.

I would like to thank them, as well as all the GRIPIC colleagues with whom I learned and taught, in particular Yves Jeanneret, Emmanuel Souchier and Caroline Marty, Valérie Patrin-Lerclec, Etienne Candel, Odile Cortinovis, Ambre Abid-Dalençon, Hécate Vergopoulous and Emmanuelle Fantin.

The ideas in this thesis are the result of conversations with Allan Bahroun, Thomas Grignon, Samuel Goyet, Pierre-Carl Langlais and Pascal Bué.

Participants in the doctoral seminar Transnum will also be sure to recognize some of the micropolitical issues discussed together.

The non-academic seminar Consequences during the struggles against the labor law reform of 2016 in France had an indirect although great influence on this research. Thanks to all the people involved in this all too rare experience.

I'd also like to thank the staff at INHA, BNF and the Robert Sabatier municipal library, who know how to make these spaces hospitable.

My final thanks therefore go to the reader. I hope that this book invites dislocation, and that certain fragments will be taken up and distorted, even if discreetly.

Introduction

When the dot-com bubble burst in the early 2000s, some venture capitalists bucked the market and continued to invest.[1] Among them was Sequoia Capital, an investment fund best known for backing Google. The firm waited and watched for a few months before entering into negotiations with the team at a video-sharing site called YouTube, which was already experiencing impressive user growth. Jawed Karim, Steve Chen, and Chad Hurley—the three founders of YouTube and PayPal alumni—knew from the start that video would be a game-changer: Karim had read an article about it in *Wired*. The team decided to experiment with the tools and formats already available. In a matter of weeks, they tried a dating site format via filmed portraits, a more comprehensive video storage server (the tagline read: Your digital video repository), and a FlickR/Delici.ous-style tool for aggregating digital videos of all kinds (upload, tag, and share!). Finally, they landed on a video publishing tool that allowed anyone who shoots or edits video to showcase their work and hopefully find an audience (Broadcast Yourself!).

Two decades on, according to a recent MIDiA survey of American audiences, 55 percent of consumers watch music videos on YouTube, compared to 24 percent who say they listen to music on Spotify. Criticized for paying too little to rights-holders, YouTube does not hesitate to point out its comparative advantage, pointing out that one-third of the revenue it gives out to copyright holders comes from the distribution of music tracks in videos produced by third parties.

Given the prominence of YouTube for contemporary music and the music business, it's easy to assume that it sprang up overnight as the result of a few initial good ideas and positive circumstances. Rather, it was the result of a long, tortuous process of trial and error. In fact, if we take a step back, we're prompted to take a very different view of the usual story of YouTube as a technological innovation that revolutionized music culture. This book is interested in exploring that reverse thesis: that is, how music played a crucial role in shaping what YouTube is. *How Music Changed YouTube* looks at how music has helped shape YouTube as a device and a platform for music publishing, listening, and media consumption in general.

In fact, if we look at the background to YouTube's creation, it's clear that that music played an important role in its emergence, stabilization, and success from the outset. At the time YouTube was launched, the peer-to-peer file-sharing pioneer Napster had just shut down. Its competitors were also closing one by one, and MySpace, the main destination of the music Web at the time, was experiencing multiple technical setbacks and a growing disaffection amongst its users. Music-lovers were looking for new ways to share files, while record companies were looking for ways to regulate the distribution of those files and, after a long period of disdain, commercial outlets for digitized music. As music helped launch YouTube, two dynamics could meet: the construction of a technical and media innovation on the one hand, and the adaptation of a set of musical formats and musical practices to an Internet-based media environment on the other. This book takes up the challenge of examining the intersection of changes in the way music functions online and the platform offered by YouTube, questioning the meeting of these two trajectories, and locating crucial moments and places in this intertwining. It aims to illuminate a key episode in the digitization of music, while offering a grounded and sometimes counterintuitive perspective on the relationships between music and platforms.

By focusing on the relationship between YouTube and music, I seek to bring to light a number of parallel and interconnected stories. The first is the capture of digital music formats by a dominant player in the Web economy, which follows the established trend of technology entrepreneurs reaching into music markets to popularize their own devices and build the value of their patents. It situates YouTube within a broader movement of the micromaterialization of music and the corporate lock-in of devices for playing and editing music (Chapter 1).

From there, I consider the evolution of the relationship between recent strategies of media capitalism and historical cultural industries, particularly the music industry. The major players on the Web regularly suggest a scenario in which their tools are supposed to disrupt the game, democratize the means of distribution, and usher in a new world in which authenticity and spontaneity align with global popularity. In the case of YouTube, we will see that the users themselves were initially happy to play a part in this narrative, but that the old guard of cultural industry monopolies quickly followed suit, helping to sustain the development of the very project that otherwise claimed to marginalize them (Chapters 2 to 4).

Finally, I will turn to a perhaps less familiar story: the construction of a new infrastructure for music copyright and the music economy. Through the symbolic and technical framing of promotional activities, as well as the introduction of new copyright control tools and audience measurement criteria, YouTube has positioned itself at the forefront of a specific market for music based on streamlined video publishing, content filtering, and advertising. Thus, while claiming to provide only logistical support and other neutral technical tools to its contributors ("creators"), the company participated in redefining the values of music in public culture. In this respect, YouTube not only evolved through its mobilization of elements and practices from (online) music cultures, but has also affected the very existence of music, at least as far as the practices on YouTube are concerned (Chapters 5 through 8).

The research behind the analysis in this book is based on a mix of disciplines and methods that I used in a first period of six years of initial research, from 2012 to 2018. My main background is in media studies, and more specifically in the sociosemiotics developed at GRIPIC (Sorbonne University) by people like Yves Jeanneret, Emmanuël Souchier and Adeline Wrona. This approach focuses on the cultural analysis of digital media/software and the social conditions of interpretation, and connects to work done elsewhere by Lev Manovich or Maria Eriksson, to name only two.

An important corpus for this work consisted of every day of the YouTube.com homepage in the period from 2005 to 2009. I accessed records of these pages thanks to the database offered by the Internet Archive through the interface of The Wayback Machine, with some cross-checking with the INA's Archives du Web in Paris. With YouTube's turn to "personalized" homepages, I looked at a wider range of screens and tools designed by the company, from YouTube for Artists to YouTube Mix. I also read extensively the YouTube blog and its offshoots, and followed the coverage of YouTube in both the mainstream international dailies (*The New York Times*, *Le Monde*) and the specialized press (*The Verge*, *Techcrunch*, etc.).

The chapter The Hit Machine Narrative discusses in more detail the advantages of a sociosemiotic approach to analyzing music videos and their meanings in a digital context. The chapters Competing for fun and The Streamlining of Expression draw on cultural studies and popular music studies, as well as the pioneering work on YouTube by the scholars who have contributed to the volume *The YouTube Reader*, and Jean Burgess and Joshua Green's book *YouTube: Online Video and Participatory Culture*. Between the writing of this book and its publication, researchers such as Stéphane Constantini, Michael L. Siciliano, Jeremy Wade Morris, Michael Spanu, and Nancy Baym have bridged the gap between YouTube's positions on music making and music promotion, which I discuss, and how musicians and labels engage with the platform in practice. There is, of course, a whole field of research to be pursued here, especially in articulating YouTube's normativity with situations and experiences that depend on, but are not limited to, class, race, gender, and geography. The final two chapters, on copyright control and audience measurement, draw mostly on sociological economics and science and technology studies. Finally, the reception of the French version of this book has highlighted the influence of more traditional strands of critical theory. Michel Foucault's genealogical approach to the relations of knowledge and power, as well as Adorno's and Benjamin's dialectical thinking about culture under the influence of technology and capitalism, have indeed left their mark on this work.

1

From Music Boxes to the YouTube Player (2000–05)

The media discourse on digital music innovation often focuses on the business ideas of entrepreneurs and the interplay of market forces, leaving out discrete but crucial design decisions. In this chapter, I will follow the inspiration of science and technology studies scholars such as Jonathan Sterne and Jeremy Wade Morris, who have emphasized the importance of multilayered studies of formats and devices. I will consider the micromateriality of music software to understand the dynamics of change in music culture and economy. This is not a way to return to a deterministic account of the power of technology, but, on the contrary, to emphasize how technical objects are themselves shaped by contradictory aesthetic, economic, and cultural logics, even when, in retrospect, they appear to be the result of a process of natural selection and evolution. I will thus show how YouTube has made the most of collective labor on recording formats and software to strategically reconstruct ways of storing, displaying, and playing music online. In the process, a branded and optimized video player has become a critical asset that has allowed YouTube to attract Internet users and take control of audiovisual document and data flows.

The Emergence of Online Listening

According to Steve Collins and Sherman Young,[1] given that music was already stored in binary code on compact discs, it was predestined to be transposed into the digital environment. They even suggest that music was the perfect guinea pig for many technological innovations. A closer look, however, reveals that this explanation is insufficient: the inscription of sound recordings into the framework of data processing and networks had to face several obstacles. At the beginning of the 2000s, all the stages of sound transduction had to be translated into hardware and software systems. The personal computer had to become a "multimedia machine" and to feature a CD-ROM player ready to play soundfiles. It would take some time for sound files to regain their value as documents and resources in their own right in the digital environment, and particularly before they were supported by a variety of websites designed for publishing, listening or sharing music.[2]

In this reformation of music's material culture, the software for playing (or listening to) sound and video files has played a major role. The ordinary and stereotypical character of media players corresponds to their underlying complexity: they are designed to make us forget their conditions of production as well as themselves – they are supposed to be 'seamless'. This listening and viewing software was initially part of the kit that came with the purchase of a computer. Other software was distributed as freeware or based on open-source elements. Stand-alone software can be reserved for sound formats, such as Apple's iTunes, or it can play sound and video interchangeably, such as the "classic" devices that were Windows Media Player (Microsoft), Quicktime (Apple), or Real Player (Real Audio). Jeremy Wade Worris emphasized how a player like Winamp, published by a company called Nullsoft, referred to three different media situations and practices: audiovisual programs and the experience of flow associated with the television set;[3] the computer as a versatile, multimedia machine that also served as office equipment; and turntables and audio systems that implied different listening postures, from dedicated, focused appreciation to distant consumption. With its syncretic design and skeuomorphism, Winamp helped to give music back its dimension as a discrete object, to make a music file not just a degraded copy of a tangible 'original', but a music recording in its own right, making it something that could be manipulated and valuable in a computer environment.[4]

After Winamp and the various desktop media player initiatives, some software engineers, Web developers, and commercial software publishers tried to bring this functionality to the Web. Casual and professional Web developers began by imitating the forms and functionalities of desktop players to reinvent them as small widgets[5], often in the Java language. They let them flourish on

Web pages, alongside small modules for displaying weather reports or stock quotes, foreshadowing mobile applications. To save programming time, they constantly exchanged code snippets and tips. The archives of their blogs show their trials and tribulations. Often, they showed themselves to be as much concerned with the idea that technical optimization can only go one way as they were with a broader poietic approach to code, wanting to make the most of the range of possibilities offered by different programming languages and standards.

At the time, their discussions centered on the proper way to display and play sound on Web pages. They were experimenting with the replacement of files that had to be downloaded before being played on a desktop player, with simple links that were visible in small players embedded in Web pages and could be activated through the Web browser. These experiments considered aesthetic, economic, and technical criteria. The community debated optimal compression rates, the best way to embed the source code in pages (via autoplay when the page loads, or via playback that requires the user to click buttons that mimic, for example, the iPod interface), the adaptation of HTML tags to Netscape or Microsoft browsers, and the choice between HTML features and third-party environments available as plug-ins, such as Active X (Microsoft) or Flash (Macromedia). Macromedia's Flash MX suite and its .SWF format—proprietary but free to use—marked a turning point, giving site editors a standard (available on 98 percent of machines[6]) to get around the compatibility problems posed by the HTML tags that typically generate players in browsers. Once standardized and integrated into development routines, Flash-based music players proliferated as ready-to-copy snippets of code on specialized websites, then as modules that users could add with a few clicks from within the leading online text-publishing tools (such as Blogger). In making this easy, the publishers of these sites and tools were all following the advice of author and consultant Nat Torkington, who, in a short insert in Tim O'Reilly's Web 2.0 manifesto entitled "A Web 2.0 investment thesis"[7] put forward the idea that "the successful companies all give up something expensive but considered critical in order to get something valuable for free that was once expensive". This principle offers a good description of how the logic of freeware and freemium would continue to expand with the strategies of free-access platforms that cover their costs by exploiting user data.

The Invention of the YouTube Player

Although there were some early experiments around video, the emergence of Web media players happened first and foremost around music. Between 2005 and 2010, many so-called MP3 blogs and aggregators such as Hype Machine became the main force in online music media.[8] Alongside peer-to-peer software and a site like MySpace, they were presented in the specialist and general press as the realization of the Web's promise of access to culture, while at the same time becoming a new emblem of so-called piracy.[9] For their part, marketing experts began to assess their usefulness in generating word-of-mouth buzz,[10] and labels began to negotiate with bloggers to release exclusive singles. On what became audioblogs, music players began to replace rather than add to the MP3 download links: by making the music available without offering it as a downloadable file, they came to represent a compromise between making the music widely available and maintaining a certain scarcity that would allow record companies to continue selling the files on online stores like iTunes.

In this landscape, while YouTube's designers drew inspiration from pre-existing sites such as the photo-sharing site FlickR,[11] the association of personal profiles with a "portal" framework, as well as the structure of the name (You/Tube), was immediately reminiscent of MySpace. The site, owned by Rupert Murdoch's News Corp, was one of the most visited at the time and one of the first important destinations for music media.[12] Like MySpace, YouTube offered Internet users the opportunity to access video-publishing tools. On another level, YouTube differed from MySpace in that all of its paths led to the media player, with the little arrow of the playback function even serving as the logo for the YouTube brand.

YouTube's designers were not content with making the player the centerpiece of the site. The embed code was placed on the site's pages, inviting users to make the recordings their own by copying them from one site to another. Despite its notorious technical flaws, MySpace had generated a rapprochement between the copy-paste of bits of code, the exchange of recordings, and self-expression or communication online.[13] But this deportalization of documents through copy and paste was also in line with the PayPal button (linked to the online auction site eBay), a fact explicitly claimed by Chad Hurley, the designer among the trio of co-founders.[14] Providing such widgets had the advantage of spreading the brand and its tools while retaining transactions and usage data. But while YouTube resembled MySpace in this respect, the two sites were still competitors. Realizing that users were mobilizing YouTube players on their sites, MySpace blocked this integration to maintain a strategic advantage.[15] MySpace then followed YouTube's lead, editing its own player format before deciding to reopen its pages to YouTube exports.[16] (Online videos from this particular period can still be found online with a little research. They feature nervous early adopters showing presentation videos shot in their bedrooms, awkwardly addressing an audience of which they seem to have only a vague understanding.)

Music offered a way for YouTube to integrate into MySpace profiles with ease, in the process allowing YouTube to build its reputation and register new users. Admittedly, the back-office forms that YouTube users had to go through to publish music recordings in/as videos did not mention sound or music specifically.[17] But a search on the keywords "audio" and "YouTube" for the year 2005 revealed several free software programs, such as Slide Trax, that offered to convert sound files into videos. Depending on one's know-how, it was thus possible to use YouTube's storage space to host musical tracks, which many Internet users did not hesitate to do (see Chapter 2). Often described in terms of a gift economy, this inclusion of music on MySpace via YouTube constituted a vector of cross-gratification, allowing Internet users to present themselves as proselytizing amateurs, all under the gaze of their favorite musicians.[18] Analogous to the display of tracks being listened to in instant messaging software such as AIM[19] or on dedicated sites/software such as Last.fm,[20] the duplication of a track nested within the YouTube player signaled cultural preference and perpetuated a portrait of the Internet user as consumer-curator, a more casual version of what would become fully fledged "music influencers."

Under these conditions, recorded music—even when it circulated for free—began to function on the Web as a quasi-commodity, or more precisely, as a commodity by destination.[21] Its circulation began to support the formation of indexes of reputation and visibility, which sometimes could be translated into professional opportunities for musicians hoping to tour or bloggers seeking to capitalize on their work as intermediaries. From 2011, new design choices led to the automation of these actions: YouTube went from offering to copy and paste an embed code (which still required selection and a minimal knowledge of code) to duplicating the underlying code with a simple click of a button: this low-cost operation was indicative of a more general trend toward streamlining online editing and publishing of text, sound and video.[22] Music and video players became little music boxes that circulated independently of their original media contexts, and the logic of sharing or exporting them from one site to another gradually took precedence over their embedding in a master document. The YouTube player became a small nomadic monad, ready to circulate without the need to look at or modify the underlying bits of code. Moving away from the world of casual webmasters curious about sound jingles, the online video/music player would eventually become a smart, fun widget that allowed anyone to distribute pieces of music with a few clicks.

At the time, YouTube was far from being the only company to build a portal and network around audiovisual formats. But in addition to its lax copyright policy, the company was notable for the way it exploited the resources offered by Flash, providing users with large storage servers, the tools they would need to intensify sharing, and its own approach to stream management ("streaming" refers here to the technical transmission of data in packets that can be read as they are received from a temporary memory). From the point of view of Internet users, the YouTube player became the equivalent of a traditional "medium" that allowed them to store, view, and even collect recordings. Paradoxically, a device associated with the ephemeral nature of the audiovisual stream began to embody the permanence of a musical format, allowing for a semiotic surplus, that is the still or moving image functioning as a seal of authentication or an additional layer of symbolic meaning not allowed by more minimalist media players. In this way, YouTube exploited the gaps between technologies (of storage and flow) and between formats (video, sound, and software) to turn its player into a tool for playing music, while at the same time limiting users' access to the materiality of music files. Not only did the company block access to other Internet users' video/music files, but its proprietary tool and recordings became inseparable in practice: it became almost impossible to manipulate a video or piece of music *without* interacting with the YouTube player at the same time. Only special software designed to "rip" the file and reconstruct the original file from the small packets of data end-to-end could separate them again; championed by users familiar with the technique, the "YouTube rip" gradually grew into a massive phenomenon that, thanks to dedicated tools and websites, would last for almost a decade. In the meantime, however, the economic, technical, and semiotic choices made around the player allowed YouTube to take a prominent position in the circulation of recordings, laying the necessary groundwork to position the company at the forefront of online music publishing and distribution.

2

Music, Incidentally (2005–09)

YouTube's privileged position in music practices was built by embedding an entire material culture into the small format of its video player. How have the availability and functions of such a medium been activated and adapted specifically for music? What happens to music when it is mobilized in tools seemingly designed for video? And how did YouTube come to specify itself, at least in part, as a medium and tool "for music"? This chapter focuses on the aesthetics and mediality of the "first YouTube" up to 2009. I argue that music has a specific status on YouTube, being *incidental*. This use of the term must be understood in a double sense. Music is ancillary to YouTube: it is not autonomous and it is not ready to be abstracted from the flow of video to be considered on its own. At the same time, music plays a specific role YouTube, which has consequences in the stabilization of its function and purpose as a tool and a medium. In any case, the role of music in early YouTube was not just something to be supplied waiting for demand. Nor was it reducible to a catalog of songs, copyrighted or not, that the YouTube founders wisely allowed on the servers to help the site gain traction. Without neglecting these factors, I am more interested in accounting for the process that simultaneously shaped the format of music on YouTube and YouTube's broader vision. Only by establishing these coordinates can we understand the specific role played by the early contributions of users and record companies, and how they both took over the site and ultimately gave YouTube its specific "cachet" or, to use Philippe Marion's term, its "médiagénie."

The Musification of Videos

In the context of musical techniques and media, sound can be considered as infra-music, designating the continuum of acoustic realities in which sound engineers and musicians shape musical works. But sound can also refer to a dimension "beyond" music, as in the tradition of avant-garde gestures that draw attention to the qualities of concrete or ambient sound that go beyond conventional musical techniques, genres, or languages. In a third and final conception, sound can remain an ambient dimension of media experience, something *inframince*, as Duchamp called the imperceptible gap between two phenomena: it remains in the realm of the inordinate, the indiscriminate, the continuum of substance. Neither inaudible nor audible as such, the condition of sound is then to remain unnoticed. One could argue that the question of what distinguishes the plans of the sonic and the musical does not arise on YouTube, insofar as the media flow we encounter there, unlike that of television, is already sequenced in autonomous units or programs. Semiotically, the frame of the player indicates a kind of content, represented by a thumbnail, and in practical terms, clicking on a page or pressing play on the player (since autoplay on video sites didn't last long) is associated with specific expectations of that content.

However, things may be a little more complicated than they seem. In order to be recognized as such, music (like images) must satisfy our expectations of what constitutes sound as such, and has to present a certain adequacy to sensory norms. Michel Chion recalls that for decades, the term *phonogénie* was used to describe the way in which certain voices and certain songs were adapted to the noise of the medium in order to allow us to grasp the style of a voice, a melody or a work as aesthetic forms.[1] This vocabulary is no longer in use, but contrary to the usual discourse about the supposed transparency of digital recordings, this does not mean that digital audiovisual formats have always been a perfect match for the notions of what we are supposed to hear. The first YouTube videos are a lesson in this regard, as they tested our expectations of what constitutes "proper" sound, which in this case means "distinct" and "intentional." Just as the first YouTube users were quick to develop specific audiovisual editing styles, including the use of jump cuts to enliven the scarcity of sets and protagonists, they also sought to develop standards for sound, seizing on the knowledge of mixing and exchanging tips. The film critic Joost Broeren reports on these early exchanges, which, if they did not achieve "good quality" (in terms of a certain idea of "professional" standards), at least sought to make recording techniques—especially the properties of microphones embedded in digital cameras, phones, or webcams—sufficiently unobtrusive: "Instead of demanding ever closer improvements to professional standards, [early YouTubers] formed a convention and approved a certain level of 'low' quality, for example through the acceptance of built-in microphones and a comparatively high tolerance for background noise."[2]

These standards of acoustic quality thus contribute to moving videos away from the aesthetics of pure capture that were initially valued highly by YouTube's founders as a way of highlighting the site's ability to host event-driven videos, whether related to events of a historical scale (Jawed Karim cites the 2004 tsunami videos as the inspiration for the site) or more ordinary surprises (the seemingly on-the-spot karaoke/dance videos, such as Garybrolsma's cover of "Numa Numa," that did much for the site's early popularity). Rather, they lead into the terrain of reflexivity towards a specific audience and specific skills in directing videos. Sound is thus involved directly—even if sometimes in spite of itself—in all the parameters that make up the YouTube style of early videos, and that helped to define what the site was for.

This issue of sound treatment has a direct impact on the forms of music presentation that have attracted the attention of researchers. Based on the rankings of the most viewed "channels," Broeren distinguishes between YouTube videos that show people lip-syncing to popular songs, covers of songs by users' favorite artists (these two categories may or may not include dance performances at home), and performances of original songs. In fact, videos focusing on song performances (without dance or comedy numbers) were almost non-existent on the home page in the early days, with the exception of Aimee Jacobsen, a young woman who claims to have twenty-five years of musical training and plays an unusual instrument, a keyboard glockenspiel. Registered since August 2005 under the pseudonym "THAUMATA", she is responsible for some of the most successful videos in the early days of YouTube, perhaps because she has always poked fun at her own performances in her choice of titles: one is "Drunken Aggression on the Keyboard Chime." It is probably with this video that many viewers were first introduced to the now recurring gimmick of a "creator" looking into the camera and introducing her upcoming song in a familiar and modest tone, explicitly inviting the viewer to get ready to listen.

Rainer Hillrichs has compared the warm reception of the THAUMATA videos to that of a local musician performing in a café or pub, without reference to professional musical standards. Another rare example was a woman calling herself Terra Naomi, who appeared in 2006 with a musical exercise presented as such, her song "Say It's Possible."[3] (She signed with Universal and then Island, but ended up self-releasing and, after a few years of touring, wrote an essay in 2015 called "How Signing A Major Record Deal Nearly Destroyed My Music Career."[4]) More famous artists like Justin Bieber and Ariana Grande also tried the format, and SB Project, Scooter Braun's agency, made sure to build their careers by focusing media attention on the charm of their early videos and their profiles as YouTube "phenomena" (which, in Grande's case, soon became one thing among many ventures on more mainstream TV channels like Nickelodeon); even if, to my knowledge, they were never picked up to be featured on the home page, this kind of recorded performance became part of the community atmosphere of early YouTube, as registered by cultural journalists like John Seabrook or Virginia Heffernan. With notable exceptions such as these, however, the videos presented by the editors in the early days of YouTube did not follow this distinctly musical format. In fact, a viewer visiting the site in the early months of its existence often had no way of knowing whether or not the video they were about to start contained sound. In many cases, the videos were silent, as the camera phones of the time did not necessarily record sound; and in the case that they did contain an audio component, it was difficult to know whether the presence of sound was intentional or not, and whether or not it was actual "music" as in an intentional recording. Sound and music, then, remained in a zone of undecidability between formlessness and form, the constructed and the accidental.

In the first weeks of the site's existence, when YouTube still presented itself as a video storage space, the home page displayed a few fragmentary keywords attached to more or less decipherable thumbnails, accompanied by sometimes vague titles that seemed more like a mnemonic device for finding a video intended more for limited sharing than for being publicized to a potentially large audience. Between April and July 2005, only two video titles on the home page suggested a possible connection to music: "Bootie Christ Dance" and "Racing with some cool tunes." Even compared to the first video shot and posted on YouTube ("Me at the zoo" by Jawed Karim),[5] "Bootie Christ Dance" seems like a monument to amateurism. In a room, between a television, a door, and a wardrobe, a young man in a tunic and leopard-print shorts moves slowly with his arms raised. His movements are somewhere between a ritual dance and the staggering gait of a drunken person, and he ends up bumping into the door. The video lasts only thirteen seconds and ends as abruptly as it began. The framing shifts during the shot, we hear the laughter of the person being filmed, captured by the camera's (or phone's?) microphone, and in the distance, muffled, a crooner's song that seems unrelated to the images playing on the television. In this anecdotal scene, where the improvised postures of a "turbulent body" (a recurrent motif among vloggers)[6] respond to the "weak" filming choices, the music is little more than a simple background noise, but it doesn't function as an autonomous, purposeful form either.

According to François Bonnet, "There is no perceived sound that does not leave a trace. Sound is not simply what one hears, it is, as soon as it exists, as soon as it leaves a trace, something more. It has functions to perform, expectations to fulfill, things to say."[7] Compared to this hypothesis, the music of "Bootie Christ Dance" is hardly a trace. Muffled by a noise artifact from the microphone and by what sounds like the cameraman's laughter, this low-intensity music does not seem to be connected to any discernible sound source in the room. In an indeterminate zone between the inside and the outside of the filmed scene, it simply passes by, and if it can be noticed at all, it is precisely because it seems absolutely alien to both the performance and the video scene.

What the camera captures in "Bootie Christ Dance" is, therefore, a spectral quality of the music, both in its deficiency and in its excess in relation to the performance "shot at home." Its functions remain mysterious; it has (almost) nothing to express, either in relation to the dancer or to the filmmaker. It has meaning only as a fleeting phenomenon. The sound mix suggests an indifference to sound, an inability to make music become discourse. Like the protagonist of the video—and we have no way of knowing whether he is choreographing his movements or simply staggering about—the barely perceptible song invites us to appreciate the parallel order of the anecdotal, how it disturbs our conception of music and the confidence of our ways of listening.

Released just days after "Bootie Christ Dance," the video "Racing with some cool tunes" illustrates this floating mode of existence in a different way. As its unusually literal caption suggests, it scrolls through "racing clips paired with some cool tunes." These notations tell us that the video contains several tracks, but once the video starts, you have to pay special attention to notice them: they are blended and mixed to best follow the montage of shots. Unlike "Bootie Christ Dance," however, the music here is fully invested. Indeed, "Racing . . ." is a deliberate mix on two levels at once: a montage of car scenes punctuated by guitar riffs, a sequence of rock songs that exist elsewhere on their own. But "Racing . . ." still has an ambiguous status, somewhere between an autonomous aesthetic resource (the "tunes") and an assemblage of sounds (a "mix"). Both "Bootie Christ Dance" and "Racing . . ." thus illustrate the particular modalities of music's presence on YouTube. Alongside the more structured videos of dubbing, cover songs, or dancing at home, music can also be barely audible, or even when it is detectible, remains in an in-between state that indirectly reveals the disciplinary character of the art of sound; it manifests how the world of forms evolves out of a continuum of sensory experience and how we learn to tune into it.

Many early YouTube contributors have taken advantage of this moment of uncertainty about the norms of expression, deliberately playing with the potential to blur them. In the months following the two excerpts mentioned above, several videos on YouTube presented the lability of sound in relation to different objects or spaces: a video like "Music drives it crazy" showed a cup visibly moving under the effect of the vibrations of loudspeakers,[8] while "The Incredible Mouth Band" scrolled through a series of instruments labeled with their names while the same voice sang each percussion sound or note.[9] While one emphasizes the tactile dimension of sound waves, the other emphasizes the acousmatic power of the recording, the auditory fiction that is always the link to a specific "sound" source. When we watch them today, these videos still play with our senses, manipulating sound and image separately, in a rudimentary and joyful exercise that indirectly recalls the aesthetics of Pop Art and avant-garde film. The lines are blurred between sound/music as background or ambience, physical manifestation and playful matter on the one hand, and as a "full" form, authorized, addressed and ready to be appreciated and valued, on the other. Experts and researchers, as well as music lovers and record aficionados, all concerned with the integrity of sound and works, tend to focus on the latter when talking about "recorded music." Beyond the scholarly interest in processes of remediation per se, attention to the margins of musical experience as they play out in the "weakest" forms of entertainment shows us what can be gained or lost when recorded music encounters new media and formats. On an initial level, these videos show that any change in format, even for the casual videographer, becomes an opportunity to express a certain reflexivity about audiovisual techniques, even if only to test their limits. But more than that, they suggest that it is always an opportunity to experiment through the metamorphoses of music and media, rather than immediately mourning the loss of stable and robust technical conventions, or hastily reconstituting them. Of course, any casual inscription of music on a video site like YouTube can certainly be interpreted as a potential departure from the reserved knowledge of editing and releasing music. But it is also part of a long tradition in which music has been associated with a variety of sensations, images, and experiments, from multimedia performance art such as opera to the ephemeral audiovisual techniques of music videos. In any case, these first uses of music on YouTube allow us to experience how music, rather than being an aesthetic reality that is immediately autonomous and obvious, can emerge as an incidental dimension of the media: in contact with new media devices such as YouTube, music is not so much radically transformed as it is first brought back to the fragile character of the norms that guarantee its autonomy.

Music Becomes Official

If music was initially only a marginal dimension of YouTube videos, how did it gain its autonomy? In the first year of the site, there was no shortage of indirect references to music. Images of instruments, appropriated album covers, and the performances of solo instrumentalists helped build an idea of music as a leisure activity. This aspect, as we well as few burgeoning signs of fan culture, could be found on the pages of "Channels," one of which was titled "Music (singing, dancing, guitars)". There we observe friendly competition among a group of aspiring video directors/producers using YouTube to gain experience. But signs of a more official culture of music production were slow to appear. And without these signs, there was no music in its most important sense—that is, as a form of expression and autonomous experience. Book historians have largely demonstrated that a certain number of signs and choices in their design were necessary to establish the singularity of a single text despite the plurality of its material manifestations, and thus to structure a horizon of aesthetic expectations around the notions of author and work. They have shown that even a format as legitimate as the book-as-codex remained relatively unstandardized for much of its history, with the position of titles and authors' names floating throughout a volume's edition or varying in spelling from one copy to another, complicating any effort at identification.[10] This problem of formatting paratext is exacerbated in the Web environment, since the Web erases the cues normally associated with the sense of touch and miniaturizes those normally detectable by the eye. If, as we have seen, the editing of a video's soundtrack is an important part of distinguishing a musical entity as such, at this point the proper names and titles of the works were one of the first and only ways for a YouTube visitor to really anticipate the presence of music as an intentional expression. It is therefore the reference to the personalities of the "music world" that, by appealing to the visitor's background knowledge, helped to transform the thumbnails and the video player box into a more or less stable documentary format, and to link them to more tangible recording formats, even if YouTube is still known today for the ephemeral character of its archives, in which navigation is challenging given the multiplication of versions and duplicates.

It would nevertheless take some time for explicit references to specific names to qualify the sound tracks of the videos and give them the more legitimate status of musical works. On the home page, music kicked off this nominalistic turn: there, the British group The Orb appears to have been the first to have adopted the convention of "artist name—song title" with a video for the song "Once More," uploaded in August 2005. They were soon followed by a Coca-Cola advertisement (the caption read "moved to tears"), and the trailer of a film by French director Claude Lelouch. One had to wait until December that year to see visible references to established musicians, the first being a competition proposed by R&B singer-producer Ryan Leslie, and the next a a live performance by neo-folk singer Devendra Banhart for *Spin* magazine.

In April 2006, YouTube made its first distinction between categories of users by introducing the role of "Director,"[11] which allowed selected users to upload longer videos, add a special logo to their pages, and have more flexibility in tagging their videos, which seemed to indicate a willingness to adapt the site to the needs of professional or semi-professional producers. Progress was maintained a few months later in July 2006 with the launch of YouTube For Musicians: the tool offered additional form fields when publishing videos, allowing users to, for example, fill in the name of a record company and then see its account appear in a dedicated "Musicians" section, prominently displayed on the home page alongside the "Featured" and "Most Recent" video rankings. While this reference to record labels seemed to signal a desire to allow record labels to post official videos of their back catalog, a message on the video-loading screen reminded users that it was forbidden to post copyrighted music: the ambiguity of YouTube's position on copyright only increased. On the one hand, this warning could be read as an incentive for Internet users to post only music they own the rights to. But a less charitable view could see it as a way for YouTube (at the time) to anticipate the risks of accusations of fraud by placing the responsibility on Internet users. YouTube may have been safer than most: the company had signed discreet deals with a few major companies in its first year of existence, and the "safe harbor" of limited liability for hosting services in the United States protected it;[12] on the other hand, the shutdown of Napster in 2002 had set a legal precedent, and no one was sure which way the wind was blowing.

As a result of the update introducing a Musicians section, the first record label to appear on YouTube.com was Sub Pop. Founded in 1986 by Bruce Pavitt, Sub Pop was known for releasing records by Nirvana and several other bands later identified as "alternative rock." Bruce Pavitt had begun his involvement in the music scene in 1980 by publishing a fanzine of almost the same name—*Subterranean Pop*—devoted to American independent labels, and selling cassette tapes through the paper. When he founded Sub Pop, he had the idea of organizing a "singles club": a subscription would allow customers to receive a 7 inch single from the label every month, thus ensuring a steady stream of income for his company. Sub Pop was thus a label for which independence meant not only distance from the majors, but also the construction of shorter distribution channels that aimed to get close to its audience, anchored in a local community of artists. Sub Pop's brand of DIY entrepreneurship might have seemed in keeping with the ethos of YouTube itself, even if it was already owned by a search giant like Google. In this case, it helped launch the single "Phantom Limbs" by The Shins, a band better known for their finely arranged pop songs and the soundtrack to the indie film *Garden State*.

In May 2007, as American television began to show interest in the site, Universal Music took its turn and released the song "Wood Grain Wheel" by rapper Slim Thug. Like The Shins in their own category, Slim Thug was an ideal candidate to experiment with a new alternative distribution method: the Houston rapper had a background in DIY distribution. His "mixtape" CDs sold cheaply in Houston, were easy to duplicate, and fueled a substantial underground economy. Now that his music was available on YouTube, users pushed the duplication logic even further. They soon extracted the song from that first video and reintroduced it elsewhere and in other forms, illustrating it, for example, with a slideshow of photos of the rapper in the manner of fan magazines. In a few years, references to professional artists were reintroduced on YouTube, approached as a means of promoting music videos and singles, but above all in relation to a history of informal economies and/or "alternative" models of marketing.

A DIY Aesthetic

In light of the above—and in retrospect—it is easy to read the dynamics of YouTube as a unilateral movement of formatting and professionalization that would gradually give way to the established actors of the record industry. Without excluding what goes along with this scenario, it should be noted that the first three years of the site's existence were marked less by the replacement of casual musicians by established artists than by an accommodation between the two. This is in line with what MySpace users and music blog readers were already familiar with: the formal equality (in both senses) between Internet users and established artists,[13] within an as-yet unstable medium, gave the site its appeal and charm, prompting dance-pop star Lady Gaga to ask YouTube's designers, a few years later to preserve its "shitty" appearance.[14]

Moreover, the common opposition between the hobbyists or non-professionals who would reveal themselves as online "creators"—and who remain at the center of sociological discussions about platforms—and the musicians who would seek to rejuvenate their promotional tactics there and/or find a way to promote themselves, deserves to be qualified more precisely. While it is easy to understand the implications of this opposition when discussing structured art worlds, there is a danger of giving an imprecise idea of the status of users who were producing, creating or promoting music during this period of YouTube's life. It is not just a matter of noticing that these video producers, like those who often express themselves on the Web, constituted a social minority. Rainer Hillrichs has gone further, claiming that almost all of the most prominent vloggers in these early days were people who were already very involved in pursuing careers in video, media and advertising.[15]

This may explain why Hillrichs discovered only one musician among the most visible channels in YouTube's first year: singer and guitarist Aimee Jacobsen, who at this time used YouTube to perform covers of hit songs in intimate settings. Contrary to YouTube's later self-image, there were few self-taught or homegrown musicians among the emblematic contributors of this period (and hardly any in subsequent years selected to be featured the site's homepage). This is not to say that music has not played a key role in YouTube's destiny, but much of its impact has come through other video styles, from the apparent "cloning" of a re-released video, to mash-ups, lip-dubs, and the most daring "remixes."

At first glance, the diversity of these video formats may seem overwhelming, but this diversity is in fact far from unfathomable. This is primarily because not all formats have the same status on the site. In fact, only some of them are selected to appear on the home pages and to play a role in YouTube's identity as a medium rather than just as an archive. Second, many of these videos cover three main and distinct modalities within the audiovisual mediation of music, even if these are sometimes combined in one video or one channel.

The first modality concerns music as a tangible recording, linked to archival culture and heritage. It includes the publication of songs by record companies (as with Slim Thug's video), but also and above all by collectors, as the essayist Mark Greif had noted in 2008, when aficionados played Blue Note jazz records in their videos.[16] The semiotic surplus that the video format could potentially add to the music is denied; instead these videos are a way to authenticate the video by linking back to an original recording (cassette, vinyl, etc), whose duration often matches the video's. In this way, the video's function is to make visible the materiality of the original recording, with references to the sonic source such as "original quality" (suggesting that the video is listened to according to logics of fidelity, authenticity, and authority), or via discographic credits (i.e label, release date, format, etc.)

The second modality deals with music as human expression and as a mode of social communication. It is typically embodied in the videos of Aimee Jacobsen, filmed in the mode of the first person facing the camera (pro-filmic) and edited to emphasize the direct communication between the singer and her audience. The third modality is undoubtedly the most specific to YouTube: it concerns the use of music as a pragmatic resource, the sound recording being, from the point at which it appears on the site, nothing but a fragment, a significant and affective unit ready to be combined and reinterpreted in an audiovisual assemblage. If the heritage modality is directed towards tradition, and the expressive modality towards the present moment of exchange, the modality we refer to as pragmatic is directed towards the future: it aims at the potential of intermediality and at the effects of the sound–image conjunction. We have seen how this modality, which encompasses the multiplicity of possibilities allowed by the logics of sampling and remixing (from explicit intertextuality to the dissolution of the source material, from semantic appropriation to the effects of quasi-synesthetic sensory intensification),[17] emerged above in the games around how sound and music were presented; but more generally, it was omnipresent in the early days of YouTube, especially as a key element in the rhetoric of vlogs.

Included in this latter registry of cobbled-together uses of copyrighted (but uncredited) music are videos promoted by the site's editors. On August 9, 2005, an insert appeared on the home page:

> August Video Contest! Can you dance? Inspired by Matt Harding, YouTube is proud to present our first monthly video contest. To enter, simply record yourself dancing in a unique location and tag the video with wherethehellismatt. The winner will be selected at the end of the month by the YouTube team. Join the contest now!

This announcement referred to a video posted on August 4, 2005 by the user account "konefku."[18] The same video was featured on the home page two days later under the title "Man Dancing" with the caption "Matt travels around the world dancing. Left his old developer job to do this," and tagged with "video," "man," "dancing," "crazy," "guy": the whole thing easily indicates another early case of an "unruly body."

By the time YouTube editors suggested this contest, another viewer had already used this video as a model, captioning it "everyone should make one like this" ("Dancing in California," August 9, 2005). Whether or not they were prompted by the initial caption, by making Matt Harding's video a model candidate, the editors making a strong statement in support of a certain type of video.

In a speech to young university graduates in 2007, Jawed Karim chose the same video to express "what YouTube is all about" and the idea that "anyone with an idea can take that idea and make it happen."[19] But this reinterpretation of Matt Harding's video is exaggerated: Harding did not wait for YouTube to make these kinds of videos and *then* post them on his own site; for him, YouTube was just another means of distributing something he was doing already. What this video means above all is that for someone like him, YouTube was less a way of "realizing" an idea (in this case, he had already found it) than of finding new outlets to make it known. The video shows Matt Harding performing choreography in which he slides his feet on the same spot in movements reminiscent of the "Running Man" steps, also called the "Melbourne Shuffle." Behind him, scenery passes like a sequence of postcards, moving from a shopping street in Beijing (China) to Times Square in New York (United

States) through the archaeological site of Angkor (Cambodia). The music used is uncredited, but one can recognize the track "Sweet Lullaby" by the French electronic music group Deep Forest, known for its inclusion on the New Age compilation *Pure Moods* (Virgin). This song uses a lullaby from the Solomon Islands, sung by a woman named Afunakwa. It was recorded by ethnomusicologist Hugo Zemp in the village of Fulinui before being released by the UNESCO on the 1973 album *Solomon Islands: Fateleka and Baegu Music of Malaita.*[20]

This first recording gives full density to the original voice (the lyrics, in Baegu dialect, are meant to comfort an orphaned child). It works like an ethnographic field recording: you can hear the light breath of the microphone and birdsong in the background. Deep Forest's musicians separated the human voice from the acoustic environment reconstructed by the ethnographic recording, added a pan flute as if to reinforce the local color, but also a full arrangement: drums, bass, synthesizer layers, backing vocals to double the main voice, and even other voices dressed up with reverb effects. During the third chorus, Afunakwa's words get lost in a linguistic mix with the backing vocals. Through this progression, what was once distinctly Afunakwa's world is now a part of several others; her voice can conjure it up at the very moment she is removed from it.

The song, chosen by Matt Harding, is thus already arranged in a logic that is both exotic and familiar enough, and somehow redundant given the list of tourist destinations and iconic sites of non-Western countries shown in the video. But that is not all: this visual parade itself is not "just anyone's" idea, but is actually reminiscent of an official "Sweet Lullaby" video, directed by Tarsem Singh and nominated for an MTV Award in 1993. The documentary database IMDb summarizes its plot this way: "A little girl rides her tricycle in front of iconic scenes from around the world."[21] Harding's alternation between himself as the sole protagonist and a variety of locations around the world is not a testament to the YouTuber's own singular imagination, but a variation on this first music video.

Harding's video also recalls the way in which non-occidental voices were mobilized in the early days of the phonograph to promote the power of recording technology to Western audiences. Through "Sweet Lullaby," this kind of transfer of an *aura* is renewed, reinterpreted, and promoted. This stereotypical way of representing otherness and diversity is, of course, congruent with the global community imaginary that regularly accompanies the promotion of technology and media. It fits particularly well into a communicative project of unifying diversity. Thus, when the editors and founders of YouTube chose the example of Matt Harding to value the creativity of "everyone" and to encourage Internet users to express themselves, they did so from a creative format that was already a triple reproduction: the amalgam of a lullaby, its exoticizing use in a piece of electronic music, and a music video awarded for its aesthetics of tourism.

Between the othering of different cultures and a pastiche of cultural industry productions, "Where the hell is Matt" plays a double game. It is the vacation film of an ordinary tourist as well as his attempt to attract attention as a director by relying on formats that have already proven themselves. The promotion of Matt Harding by YouTube editors is therefore to be interpreted less as a recognition of the originality or spontaneity of a casual Internet user than as the result of a consensus on ethical and aesthetic conventions already well established within the cultural industries.

Without denying the potential diversity of published videos, or claiming that one video is more representative than another, Matt Harding's video reveals one of the main ways in which music takes on meaning on YouTube. The video borrows the aura and expressiveness of an original without any obvious reference to consistency or integrity, as neither Hugo Zemp, Afunakwa, nor Deep Forest are credited. The song used in the video literally functions as a piece of music, a significant fragment that is more than a sample (since it imbues the entire rhetoric of the video) while being clearly detached from any specific reference.

A little over ten days after the release of "Wherethehellismatt," another first-person video based on a hit song showed a different relationship to authorship. The video in question, titled "Summer Homework" and posted by user AsoBit, is based on the song "The Clapping Song (Clap Pat Clap Slap)," performed by Shirley Ellis—the only person credited in the caption—which was written by Lincoln Chase, arranged by Charles Capello, and released on Congress in 1965.[22] "The Clapping Song" actually adapts the lyrics of a 1930 song by the

Light Crust Droughtboys, "Little Rubber Dolly," a recording of a nursery rhyme that already existed in several variations in the United States.

The video plays ironically both with the maternal morality ... and with what Shirley Ellis' single adds to it, namely a question-and-answer game that invites the listener to clap his or her hands in time to the chorus. The irony of the nursery rhyme is reinforced in the video by scenes of a teenager running away from his homework and hanging out in his room. The rhythmic play of the song is both reconstructed and deconstructed by the quasi-synchronization of the editing: in each shot, the cut falls more or less on the beat (in a kind of audiovisual "prosody" in response to the rhythmic "stature" of the song), but this tonic accent of the cuts ultimately turns out to be empty, since the laziness of the teenager in the image, slumped in incongruous positions or holding a video game controller, represents the opposite of the vigor demanded by the singer.

This video deserves to be described in such detail because it not only uses the song as a soundtrack, but also responds to it, creating a reinterpretation and a cover in its own right. Although there is nothing to suggest that its maker intended it to stand as a work in itself, or to pose as an artist himself, the video's intertextuality and intermediality make it function as a continuation of the series of transformations of the original nursery rhyme, applying the same kind of process of addition and micro-shifting that "The Clapping Song" already did in relation to "Little Rubber Dolly".

The real irony of this video is that it was the first to introduce a reference to music copyright on YouTube, when in fact it referred to a particular American musical folklore with no clear owner. It is difficult to know whether these early instances of video covers or remixes directly inspired YouTube editors when it came to promoting the creativity of Internet users, but they are part of what has become a massive phenomenon of video covers based on facial expressions, postures and dances designed to be imitated, which has since been promoted by specialized music marketing agencies such as Dance On[23] and dedicated platforms such as the now-defunct Vine and more recently, TikTok.[24]

The first YouTube videographers to really use music for its effects in their videos manifested a particular relationship to music, using songs that were certainly from the music industry, but also indirectly linked to popular music cultures in general, with covers based on logics of proximity and shared references with the audience. Whether a nursery rhyme or a lullaby, these songs corresponded to the rewriting of a folklore inscribed in everyday life, whether in the United States or on islands in the Pacific. The registers of intimacy and ritual were thus integrated with musical "hits" enriching the meaning of expression in the video.

The first videos "chosen" by YouTube were based on syntheses between different relationships to music, captured in its relationship to other media such as television, to local and transnational spaces, to everyday life and to collective memory: the sounds heard in "Sweet Lullaby" only intensify the dialectic of the universal and the local, carried by the visuals; Shirley Ellis's voice crosses media and generations and is loaded with irony. By contributing to the circulation of the chosen songs, these videos manifest the capacity that hits already have to thematize their own circulation.[25]

Music, in the first videos presented on YouTube, is made up of fleeting clues, ready to circulate and to be altered, confused, or dissolved in the cheap spectacles of individual lives, whether made of boredom or enthusiasm, of ordinary decorations or touristic landscapes. At the same time, these videos glorify the way in which recorded music, as a standardized and industrial form as well as a repertoire of emotional nuances, participates in collective culture, defining the contours of both the anecdotal and the spectacular.

3

Competing for Fun (2006–13)

As we have seen, the first music videos selected for YouTube did not come out of nowhere. The teams that edit YouTube had increasingly drawn on this media understanding of popular music as a common resource. They did so in at least three ways: by taking advantage of the success of videos that were part of entertainment formats, musical or not, just as variety shows had become successful on television; by relying on the entrepreneurial spirit of the music industry and on nominal references to an "underground" in order to establish promotional partnerships with some major media companies; finally, by organizing their own contests and prize lists in the manner of MTV, while trying to adapt standard selection categories in an effort to enhance the spontaneity and supposed originality of the encounter between musical culture and online audiovisual creation.

From Vaudeville to *Oprah*

In the second half of the nineteenth century, the French term "variétés," originally used for a collection of literary fragments, conceived a specific trans-media format of entertainment, understood as "a program, [a] show composed of different numbers (songs, sketches, dances, music hall numbers), generally unrelated to each other."[1] Gradually, variétés came to mean a series of heterogeneous numbers and the art of combining them in a music-hall show, with an emphasis on novelty and comedy.[2] YouTube's way of combining comedy numbers and music in its "programming," or the way users associate them in certain videos, can be read as an extension of this classical tradition of entertainment.

Several of the videos most often cited as turning points in YouTube's progress toward a wider audience are, in fact, stunts that recall the variety acts' emphasis on virtuosity, humor, the wacky, and the spectacular, whether it is a music-free skit like the video "Extreme Mentos & Diet Coke" (the unleashing of a geyser of Coca-Cola, part chemistry experiment, part prank[3]) or a novelty song like "Chocolate Rain" (showcasing Tay Zonday's amazing voice-modulation skills). A channel like "Epic Rap Battles of History," featuring duels between intellectuals in a parody of rap battles, has also been one of the biggest successes in this vein.[4] More broadly, and as Henry Jenkins has noted,[5] many of the videos presented in the mainstream media as representative of what is posted on YouTube[6] continued the spirit of vaudeville, a term whose original definition refers either to the musical sense of "a song with rhyming verses and choruses based on a well-known and popular tune, which was originally a drinking song and then a satire on persons or events of the day," or in the theatrical sense of the humorous number and "small light comedy," originally "mixed with ballets and songs to a popular melody, played especially at the fair theater."[7]

One of the first videos posted on YouTube to achieve widespread media success outside of the site is a great embodiment of this combination of a tradition of familiar songs and comic performances. "Evolution of Dance" (April 6, 2006) is an excerpt from a show in which comedian Judson Laipply mimes a variety of more or less outrageous dance crazes.[8] As in most of his shows, which usually feature a single protagonist working around a single leitmotif in a short form, Laipply tries out a variety of choreographies in succession on the same stage—as if in a reverse echo of Matt Harding's video, which featured the same choreography in different locations. It begins with a rock'n'roll to an Elvis Presley song and ends with a series of poses associated with a succession of R&B hits. This pseudo-natural history of dance, in which the accumulation of steps plays with both excess and a nod to consensual references, is in fact a rereading of the history of dance on television, a common heritage as defined by the media industry.

Major US television shows, such as *Oprah*, picked up the video for prime-time exposure, framing it as a YouTube phenomenon: "The most viewed YouTube video of all time, I mean of all time, has been viewed, unbelievably,

60 million times, and it's just one man, one stage, one spotlight, look at that."[9] In just a few words, the host weaved the relationship between YouTube and a video made with an apparent economy of means, which in turn contrasted with the expensive apparatus that characterized a show like *Oprah*. The media elite thus paid tribute to the margins of the entertainment economy. The aesthetics of sampling mentioned earlier (Chapter 2) is expressed fully in Laipply's video: these are short parodic excerpts that tended to place the video within the legal tolerance of fair use (i.e., legal exceptions to copyright law such as parody or short quotation)[10] and made it an ideal candidate for promoting YouTube.

They offered both the appeal of a certain recognizable (musical) culture (to a certain idea of a general, average public) and the security of a video without copyright infringement. When viewed on YouTube, the video bridged the gap between the site's familiar "unruly bodies" or "home dances" and the American entertainment history. It can thus be read as an unintentional symbol of the end of a "golden age" in YouTube's history, that is, the end of YouTube as an outsider media company—a view, of course, based on a partially fantasized sense of its beginnings that placed it outside of market logics.[11] It represents a full loop, with the music-hall show in front of a small audience, based on the audiovisual culture of dance in fashion (dance crazes), ending up on television via a detour through a platform that presents itself as an alternative to television. In the process, YouTube took its place in a broader media landscape as a reservoir of new candidates for fame. After the Matt Harding video, it was the turn of this most recent instance of what was presented as a "YouTube success" to reveal itself less as a "revelation" of outsider talent finding an outlet on the platform than as a more familiar and predictable form of what works as mainstream TV entertainment.

A Prime-time "Underground"

YouTube's status as a talent spotlight has been associated with music as much as with comedy shows or homegrown funny videos. It was in this spirit that YouTube first featured "Videos of the Day" on its home page, and early on offered numerous contests and sweepstakes, like the one Matt Harding won. Some of these brand-sponsored videos were part of a larger series of initiatives aimed at advertisers around the same time. The *New York Times* reported in 2006 that "YouTube has been experimenting with what are essentially on-demand ads—ads on the home page with links to sponsors' videos. And [the site] allows advertisers to create custom 'channels,' collections of videos in any combination of low-key or aggressive promotion. A new video for Burger King, for example, features rap star Diddy ordering a Whopper."[12]

On September 21, 2006, YouTube launched a contest called "YouTube underground" in partnership with telecom operator Cingular Wireless, a subsidiary of AT&T Group. The metaphor of the underground has roots in Black counter-culture[13] and, in Europe, in resistance to Nazism. Usually, the term is used to denote minority, nonconformist, or rebellious ways of life and of doing music, and suggests a stratification of social and aesthetic spaces based on differences or antagonisms of values, without always being clear whether this is a de facto position, an imposed one, a chosen one, or a mere claim.

When YouTube was referring to the underground, it was promoting subcultural legitimacy[14] while promoting a contest linked to the brand of a major telecommunications company. The contest was billed as a "quest to find the most talented and entertaining self-produced musicians and bands out there." The instructions seemed straightforward, but the required criteria revealed specific expectations: "Submit videos that best represent your band's skills as musicians, songwriters, and video directors."[15] When it came to music, the company favored the multi-talented multimedia team over the expected figure of the home-studio musician. There were four categories in the contest: "best song;" "best video;" "best live performance;" and "most creative." The contest rules were even more specific about the latter:

> During the voting period, site visitors will be invited to vote for their favorite entry, taking into account the following judging criteria to determine the finalists: (50%) inventiveness and (50%) entertainment value.[16]

This meant that everyone was invited to vote, but the votes followed predetermined criteria of value and left the final decision to "qualified judges" who had to choose from among the twenty candidates with the most votes, their choice being branded "Discovery"—with this use of words, the result of a specific electoral system, limited in scope, was freed from these contingencies and the selected artist was presented as a direct result of the public's choice, and even a revelation of its taste.

By presenting itself as a space to nurture new talent, YouTube went beyond the simple role of coordinating user submissions. By supporting ways of producing and releasing music, the company aimed to become both a breeding ground for aspiring artists and their springboard to recognition. In this example, the winner of the contest got to appear on the television show *Good Morning America*: proof, if it were needed, that the underground here was not understood as a "secret" culture, nor as a movement in search of alternative forms of life and expression, autonomous or antagonistic to the mainstream.[17] Rather, it was seen as the condition of those who are still at the bottom of a ladder of visibility and who have not yet been favored by prime-time television. Under these conditions, self-produced and self-published artists are seen as musicians who can only hope for the widest possible recognition. The ambiguities of the underground no longer exist: here it is a simple lack of notoriety and visibility in a homogeneous cultural universe based on emblematic images, sounds, and situations, a specific version of the idea that was the only one that made it possible to bring together New York, indie rock, YouTube and a TV.

For American popular music scholar Emily Dolan, "indie has value precisely because it appeals (or appears to appeal) to a smaller, elite segment of society. And yet [...] indie rock sells well as a slightly exotic 'other.'"[18] The idea of "indie" evolved as the majors signed distribution deals with most of the so-called independent labels, including those that had structured themselves to avoid this situation[19]: indie then became a subset of the majors' distribution networks,[20] while still serving as a term used to designate original styles when they finally appeared on radio and television. Aesthetic and social keywords such as "underground" and "indie" not only distinguish styles, social milieus, and modes of organization; they are also constructed in a dialectical relationship with the media and commercial devices that participate through them in the dynamization of aesthetic practices, tastes, record releases, and, ultimately, the music market itself.

YouTube Underground, with its references to rap or indie rock, allowed YouTube to consecrate self-produced artists: the winners were relatively unknown to the public and specialized music media. YouTube thus negotiated a respectable distance—neither too far nor too close—not only from the major television networks, whose complicity had been established, but also from the music industry in all its diversity. These references allowed YouTube to place itself in the symbolic polarization organized within the music industry according to the dependence on the rules decreed by the majors. From this point of view, "self-production," "underground," and "indie" were all symbolic resources to be mobilized for the affirmation of YouTube's own identity as a media platform.

After the *Good Morning America* show with the competition winners, a report was published on the YouTube blog. It took the form of a short story that highlighted the complicity between the bands, as well as between the bands and YouTube, during the trip organized for the TV program. The author of the post, writing in the first person and signing only with his first name, compared the moments he had just experienced to "the old days of rock 'n' roll, when bands were friends and played together all the time, not like today where it's every man for himself": a reference that is probably less relevant to the real rock 'n' roll years than to the downtown New York scene of the early 1980s, or at least the image that a show like *TV Party*, co-hosted Chris Stein of the band Blondie, tried to convey. Here, a past was reinvented around warm fraternal feelings invoked to legitimize the present. Drawing on the similarities between artistic and technological utopias from the counterculture of the 1970s, the story was one of affinities and shared interests between engineers-entrepreneurs and musicians, at the very moment when the former were organizing the competition between the latter.

By appealing to a general audience as well as referencing underground, urban, and indie cultures, YouTube staged a deliberate distance from the music industry at the very moment it offered to guide musicians toward exposure on television.[21] Words that in music culture usually mean ideological opposition, organizational autonomy, and stylistic originality were mobilized here in a revised talent-show format that offered a peripheral path to prime time.

Popular Culture Redux

After YouTube Underground, the platform took its collaboration with the music industry a step further. The contests became more sophisticated PR operations: YouTube went from running contests to hosting its own media ceremonies. The first YouTube Awards were launched and announced to the press in March 2007: the idea was to reward the best videos of the previous year, in all categories, from a selection of nominees once again chosen by the site's editors. There were directors and actors of sketches and vlogs, but also musicians such as OK Go and Terra Naomi. The ceremony worked the other way around from YouTube Underground: this time, the editors chose the nominees, and then Internet users were invited to vote.

This system was criticized by writer and journalist Virginia Heffernan in the *New York Times*.[22] She focused first on the analogy between competition and democracy proposed by the site's editors. She criticized the privilege given to videos typical of what is posted on YouTube, and to "talent" already recognized as such by the site's regulars, in the selection of nominees. In essence, she criticized YouTube for taking a stand in favor of certain productions rather than simply acting as a neutral mediator; in short, for betraying the promises of equal voice suggested by the slogan "Broadcast Yourself!":

> The award winners, announced yesterday, will be recognizable as YouTube veterans, and their selection here makes blindingly clear the site's slacker aesthetic (Smosh, OK Go and the Wine Kone); its mush politics (the Free Hugs Campaign); and its chronic oscillation between absurdism ("Ask a Ninja") and emo ("Say It's Possible").
> This value system is not intrinsically worse than the one that determines prime-time television's crisp, white-collar aesthetic; its mainstream politics; and its chronic oscillation between punchy and sappy. It's just that YouTube's not really supposed to have any aesthetic or ideological principles, is it?

But later in the piece, the journalist abandoned this ideal of neutrality and her accusations. In turn, she marked a clear preference, in this case for the bedroom setting and rock aesthetic of the young singer Terra Naomi:

Terra Naomi with her heartbreaking "Say It's Possible" won best music video here. That's a wonderful choice. The song has got a sustained ache to it, and the visual setup for the video — the singer at the guitar crowding the camera, before an unused keyboard — is painterly, in the tradition of the best YouTube bedroom guitar videos. (Unlike the funny OK Go guys on their treadmills; I like their pluck, but it's too MTV for YouTube.) With the look of a young Keith Richards, Terra Naomi is the only girl cool enough to make the cut in the YouTube awards.

The singer's appeal to Heffernan is visible through signs of "typical YouTube" projected authenticity—as evidenced by Heffernan's contrasting her with OK Go, who were deemed "too MTV." After rejecting the focus on DIY aesthetics, Heffernan embraced it. More generally, music appeared in her article as a domain where listeners' critical sensibilities could meet their taste for competition and ranking practices. This taste for competition through voting, as a procedure that justifies meritocratic values, soon extended outward, with YouTube's intervention in institutional politics (with voter-registration campaigns or its participation in animating presidential debates in partnership with CNN),[23] as well as within the site's own perimeters, with a voting system applied to comments under videos.

The mobilization of a certain media culture of music thus extended the ways in which YouTube sought to mobilize or recreate a public opinion based on the appeal to personal preferences and the valorization of individual choice as such, regardless of domain. Music facilitated the naturalization of this evaluation culture insofar as it has often been able to carry with it, perhaps more readily than humor or dance, certain habits of classification, judgment, and distribution of merit.

In any case, YouTube's position as an authority on contests was at odds with its own promises of visibility for all. One answer to this difficulty was for YouTube to multiply the contests, the genres involved, and the judging criteria, in music or other areas, in order to perpetuate the idea that all one has to do is wait for (and work toward) one's turn or opportunity. Another answer would be to rely more on emerging artists or artists from certain musical worlds and genres that were less represented in the dominant media, to turn them into signs of approachability for more casual users.

Such a principle of playing with the margins was already at work in television at the same time, with talent shows like American Idol.[24] There, the behavioral and sartorial stereotypes of punk or hip-hop offered an image of apparent diversity in contests based on relatively narrow criteria of vocal performance. On YouTube, this diversification affected the contests themselves: after indie rock, YouTube decided to tackle rap with "On The Rise" (2007). Recognized rappers selected the winners from a pre-selection made by Internet users, but which applied only to the accounts of users who were able to access paid affiliate status. Artists like Moby or the now-forgotten New Young Pony Club also used a special corner of the site—the Communities page—to create their own challenges, often inviting users to suggest productions with a DIY aesthetic. Jens Schröter has noted the contradiction between the reference to "community" and the ubiquity of such contests.[25]

Beyond simple competitions, the company began to hold awards ceremonies in the vein of legacy media. The ceremonies demonstrated a concern for cultural authority that was no longer simply a matter of motivating a pool of video artists and musicians. In doing so, YouTube positioned itself within the annual schedule of cultural prescription organized around retrospectives, once again proposing specific criteria. But before fully embracing this model, the company first experimented with the principle of live television shows, MTV-style. On this occasion, it paired the videographers and musicians who contributed to the site with well-known performers in the same live show. YouTube Live (November 22–3, 2008) was billed as an event celebrating "the most innovative, inventive, and buzzworthy videos and people." The event was produced by Salli Frattini, who produced the MTV Music Video Awards from 2001 to 2005. It featured music celebrities such as Katy Perry, described as "music's top rising star," and singers who first found success online, such as Tay Zonday (whose mannered, mimicry-based singer-pianist act had caught on with 4chan members, who made pastiches of it)[26] and guitar virtuoso Funtwo, along with "bedroom vloggers, hilarious comedians, and elite athletes."[27]

The online magazine *The Verge* described the event as a variety show that turned into a disaster: singer Katy Perry, who was invited to host the show, mistook the livestream event for an awards show when she talked about the "YouTube Awards," and she clearly had no regard for the Internet video-makers invited to the show. Gathering new celebrities and rising stars of the music industry at one event required some adjustments, and *The Verge* noted that by April 2011, almost all archives of the performances had disappeared from the site.[28]

From then on, a kind of back-and-forth was established between YouTube, which acted in order to get closer to the music industry, and the latter, which borrowed the forms perceived as typical of an online vernacular web culture. This entanglement was reflected in the very forms of some of the videos: the efforts of Internet users to imitate the standards of the music industry and the professional worlds of entertainment were matched by the growing references to vernacular web culture in the work of musicians.

According to *The Verge*, in 2008 YouTube was still "the new kid on the block," "next to a dominant MySpace and a rapidly expanding Facebook."[29] Part of the sales pitch to attract and keep record labels—Warner had left the deal before returning[30]—was to offer a statistical analysis tool, YouTube Insights (October 2008). The tool, which had just been made available to the public, was presented by a YouTube representative at MIPCOM, an entertainment industry conference. With the help of indie rock stars from the band Weezer, Chad Hurley presented the tool as having already proven effective for market research:

> The products and features being developed by online video providers continue to evolve. For example, the American rock band Weezer launched its "Pork and Beans" video on YouTube, resulting in over 4 million views in just two days. Using our sophisticated analytics tool, the band was able to look deep into the video's views. This data provided a sort of consumer panel, allowing them to prepare more effective and powerful marketing campaigns. It even helped Weezer understand where their videos were being watched and prepare for their future tour.[31]

The video for the song in question, "Pork and Beans,"[32] was actually a compilation of other videos posted to YouTube by users that shared the aesthetic traits of "authenticity" and simple fun, and that had already achieved some success. Weezer thus celebrated the fact that its "community" could benefit from the group's notoriety, while at the same time transforming itself into a versatile public relations agent, encouraging a wider contingent of professional artists and labels to use YouTube.

This marked an important phase in a series of regular invitations from YouTube executives to the audiovisual and cultural industries. The first agreements with Italy's RAI or CBS[33] were followed by various initiatives with Hollywood and television producers, such as a first project to finance new and exclusive programs for YouTube in 2011 (led by ex-Netflix executive Robert Kyncl).[34] Among these initiatives, a budget had been dedicated to the financing of exclusive channels in collaboration with well-known personalities such as Madonna, a regular in commercial partnerships since her collaboration with the Pepsi brand in the 1980s.[35]

Despite the failure of the YouTube Live trial, YouTube launched the YouTube Music Awards (November 3, 2013) with Vice Media and Sunset Lane Entertainment as executive producers and Kia Motors as a sponsor.[36] The name itself was obviously a nod to the MTV Music Awards. This event once again served as an opportunity for the company to demonstrate its strength as an institution in the music world. But this time, the company positioned itself as a judge capable of distinguishing between music celebrities, beyond just the artists who had featured only on YouTube. The artists were selected in categories that reflected YouTube's specific logic both as technology and media provider: Video of the Year, Response of the Year, YouTube Phenomenon, YouTube Revelation, and Innovation of the Year.

This list presented YouTube as a music medium in its own right, and at the same time as a space where music was associated with certain values. Indeed, it established YouTube's claim to host and promote certain types of videos in particular (YouTube Phenomenon, Innovation of the Year), each term referring to composite statistics and rankings, but reformulated in the emerging language of online media success. The various practices were presented as "engagement." They were associated with a particular status of user-listener, the "fan," whose activity was always presented as a variation of a direct vote; even remixes, which could elsewhere be read as reinterpretations, parodies, or simply transformations of the context of an original material, were assumed to be proof of fan devotion. Consequently, the only thing left to do was to measure the importance of this fan activity: "fan engagement," "most viewed, most shared, most liked, with the most subscriptions," "best fan remix, parody or response video," "video that generated the most fan videos." As anticipated in the ceremony's video announcement, which featured high-definition music video footage, and as confirmed by the list of nominees, the YouTube Music Awards almost exclusively rewarded musicians already famous on other platforms, with "Epic Rap Battles of History" and "ThePianoGuys" being rare exceptions.

The ceremony was also an opportunity for YouTube to embrace the tried-and-true forms of legacy media like MTV, while asserting its own distinctiveness. Among the series of live performances, one in particular illustrated this dual approach: Arcade Fire's concert with actress Greta Gerwig. These personalities were not chosen at random: Arcade Fire had achieved a rare double success as a band with both "indie" critics and a more general audience thanks to their 2004 album *Funeral*, which mirrored how *Pitchfork* magazine had reached a position of influence outside the indie scene (see Chapter 6). Greta Gerwig, for her part, was already a rising figure within the emerging New York mumblecore film scene, with its semi-improvised scenes depicting the daily lives and boredom of characters in their twenties or early thirties, always on the verge of atony.[37] The actress, who co-wrote several of these films, had expanded her audience with the success of *Frances Ha* (directed by Noah Baumbach in 2012), in which she played the character of a young woman, adrift, who eventually finds success with her incongruous choreography. Gerwig's performance mobilized the ethos of both the actress and the character. In the scene, she left a small apartment, with awkward dance moves elevated to the rank of style, to reach a fairy-tale forest. After a few moments, she "broke the screen"—or rather, the fourth wall: she left what turned out to be a theater set and took the camera into a room full of spectators, where she continued her number by imitating the song in karaoke mode. Because she acted there both as a performer—a dancer on stage imitating the song—and as a projected figure of the audience, but also did not belong to the band, who we could briefly catch playing the song in the background, her performance functioned as a compromise between the two inverted regimes of the professional show and the approximate imitation of the fan doing his own number.

This video took up the variety show/vaudeville logic of mixing numbers within the same performance. By bringing together stars from different disciplines and different types of shows, it embodied YouTube's overarching ambition as well as its positioning alongside a certain kind of emerging artist. Greta Gerwig represented an emerging figure in American cinema, Arcade Fire had enjoyed a meteoric rise to fame a few years earlier, and last but not least, the ceremony was filmed by Spike Jonze, already an Arcade Fire collaborator and a filmmaker with his own reputation, first as a skateboarding videographer and then as an auteur of original music videos, who helped build the legitimacy of the format.[38]

By casting someone like Greta Gerwig, the YouTube teams were relying less on a form of otherness that they would have to deal with, and more on a young actress whose character lived a precarious life on the margins of the artistic worlds that made her a bohemian icon. Through her, the company was able to publicly project the fantasy that it regularly presented as the fantasy of its users: that of already being on the launchpad to success. In doing so, it once again defended the idea that everyone is worthy of "making it," regardless of their flaws. Greta Gerwig embodied the possibility of a new entertainment culture that fed off a musical culture that seemed far from the mainstream (even working against it), but which was still very close to it, because here, as in other instances, we were witnessing precisely how the mainstream could be rejuvenated by incorporating what was on its fringes.

Through these ceremonies, these competitions, and their successive iterations (we should also mention YouTube Rewind, modeled on the year-end reviews of the cultural press), the YouTube editors ultimately sought to present the site as the ultimate space of the popular. In doing so, they built on all the ambiguities and historical layers of popularity as a social imaginary: the myriad nuances between the anecdotal and the surprising, the minority and the marginal, generic centrality and media visibility. For YouTube, becoming an institution that defines the popular meant a specific path of legitimation that aimed down, appealing to "ordinary people," the fans from whom stars in the music industry reaped their success; but it also meant building a kind of legitimacy based on hierarchical systems of elections or competitions, thus reproducing the principle of inequalities of merit and scenographing mass appeal as a superlative achievement. As a result, a small number of musicians and artists were consecrated as exceptional, their success transcending social and aesthetic stratifications, as mediated by the orchestrated separation between "legacy" and "new" media. In this way, YouTube partially took on the expressions and signs of two different ideals of the popular, establishing its specific conjunction of vernacular/folklore and spectacle, unexpected talent and dominant culture, originality and consensus.

4

From Choosing to Streaming (2008–14)

Through various contests and media events, YouTube had demonstrated a partial commitment to the vernacular, the unusual and the ordinary, the minority and the marginal, while portraying itself as a bridge back to the universal, the central, the best, and the most visible. This construction of popularity through event formats and media rituals would soon be combined with a site redesign. YouTube undertook to rationalize the presentation of videos in order to promote its new mission: "to help discovery." To this end, YouTube also built a system of "recommendations"—which I prefer to call "soft prescriptions"—and finally to deploy a full range of branded tools (playlists, trends, and "YouTube Mix"). Once again, we will see that the metamorphoses of music on YouTube were directly related to those of the platform itself. YouTube gradually moved from a more or less unstable and polyphonic archive space to a streamlined and smoothed interface. This new design included the mediation of music, highlighting the site's ability to optimize music consumption for short-term efficiency.

The Design of Choice

As if to keep the promise of unity conveyed by the references to the vaguely defined "you," the YouTube.com home page was gradually redesigned and smoothed out. Of course, the home page has always been just one of many ways to visit the site and browse the video collection, alongside direct access to the video pages or keyword search. However, as the site evolved, the strategic investment in this page became increasingly important: it was no longer just about embodying the site's promise or providing a first glimpse of the videos available, but about keeping users coming back for more.

In this respect, this work was in line with the traditional work of commercial designers, including those of brick-and-mortar stores and especially the classic department stores. David Chaney reminds us that they knew how to give these spaces an "ethereal character, detached from contingencies [. . .] maintained by the general absence of means of telling the time, by the usually total exclusion of natural light and other elements of the external environment, and often by extremely disconcerting indications and signposts that make the visitor seem dazed, almost hypnotized."[1] This design of seduction and attention meant that videos were classified less and less as documents associated with a caption and presented more and more as commodities whose icons and names now shimmered against a smooth background. Their value was thus produced and anticipated through the optimization of thumbnails, the official or incentivizing tone of video titles, the "number of views" with which they were credited, and finally the replacement of the news column by a mosaic frame, forcing immersion in video content while framing it in a new visual phantasmagoria of free access and free choice.

At the same time, YouTube was constantly changing its claims and the range of its formats as a medium. For example, the company recharacterized its mission to its users around "discovery." Helping (or "facilitating") "discovery" became a claim that was constantly reiterated and adjusted over the years, as well as expressed through several successive redesigns of the YouTube home page, with a note on YouTube's official blog. To this end, YouTube's official blog posts explained each new feature and module with a choice of words somewhere between an instruction manual and a disarming openness and cordiality that, again, could be traced back to the very beginnings of advertising culture.

From 2008 to 2014, YouTube announced on its blog at least six times that it was repositioning the site around discovery: first, YouTube would be about "discovering great videos" (February 26, 2008), but "knowing where they're from and why we think you'll like them" (March 25, 2009); then the emphasis was on "great channels" to "explore" (January 26, 2012), which implied an attitude of involvement on the part of the user; then the subscription feature, which implied a more "receptive" attitude of sorting through what comes in. Finally, all of this consolidated around the highlighting of "new music", which coexisted with "your old favorites", and with the invitation to use YouTube to "let go" (December 11, 2014).

The music served to further YouTube's missions and claims, while the design models continued to slide, gradually moving from an emphasis on the pull of search to one on the push of subscriptions. These shifts notwithstanding, the same figure of the ideal user emerged, essentially reduced to an attitude: a vague curiosity for videos to "like," a task that was still considered to require too much effort on his part, and that YouTube, as a good adjunct, proposed to make more convenient, even to the point of making the choices and suggesting that the user let himself be carried along. The notion of discovery, which still unified these trials and tribulations, meant that YouTube didn't have to distinguish and choose between the initial attitude of this curious Internet user, involved in a research process, and the multiple strategies subsequently adopted to put her in a position of potential responsiveness to a pre-given offer, a set of strategies that began with subscriptions to channels before being extended quickly to "recommendations."

A Soft Prescription

The rise of claims around "discovery" can be read as a way of counterbalancing the universalist rhetoric that has been a staple of mainstream media, including YouTube, always at risk of being perceived as too boring and consensual. After investing heavily in promoting and defining a collective taste and video culture in its early days, YouTube has increasingly privileged the scale of individual preferences.

After Amazon, YouTube was one of the early champions of the supposedly predictive (and realistically prescriptive) system called collaborative filtering in the field of online cultural consumption. The lexical field of "discovery" seemed apt for a company that wanted to value the "personal" tastes of its users, while at the same time indexing them according to what others had chosen to watch in order to maximize the chances of clicks: what was displayed in the formulation of "personalized recommendations" as a means of deepening individual choices was, in fact, connected to the videos most consulted by other Internet users. After years of cultural critique of algorithmic filtering, it is now clear that the promise of a co-construction of the offer between a singular user and the platform does not make the principle of cultural prescription disappear. Rather, it complicates the understanding of the criteria for ranking and displaying videos, which constitutes a kind of soft prescription. In fact, qualifying the presentation of a video that has never been consulted as a "recommendation" means attributing to specific ranking systems the qualities of a deliberate and benevolent dialogue between people concerned with communicating a taste, even if it is rather a process of statistical aggregation and approximate matching of the data logs left by online behavior.

Through the vocabulary of recommendations, YouTube has thus embraced the ethos of the curator or peer who benevolently shares cultural references, while this kind of inter-individual exchange has been marginalized in its own design (for example, even at the very beginning, a subscribe button was always more prominent than direct messaging links, and the latter were quickly removed). While contemporaneous streaming services like the now defunct Daisy had offered rudimentary experiments in algorithmic sorting, and experts have called for more open and interactive systems, YouTube also excludes any such intervention. In fact, the company removed the mentions that explained the criteria and sources of specific recommendations not long after they were first introduced.

Instead, recommendations became a way to encapsulate the paradoxical presupposition of a general desire for music, rather than a specific taste. YouTube established a relationship to music that was reduced to a need to be (easily) satisfied before any evaluation and judgment could form[2]: the emphasis was on a "lean-back" (*sic*) posture on the part of the user/listener.[3] To a lesser extent, this automation of the browsing activity anticipated part of each user's reflexive relationship to their own sensibility, in order to guide them toward a posture of mere reaction to supposedly adequate suggestions, as opposed to queries and inquiries in the site's database.

Of course, this is a design scenario, and reflexivity is not something that media can easily eradicate; however, features that shape the user's browsing environment and technical design play a role by making resources more or less accessible in order to sustain such an attitude. In this sense, YouTube as a device discourages users from searching in a way that makes sense to them by trying to guess what they might want: "recommendations" function as procedures of pseudo-serendipity and take priority over a more voluntaristic curiosity, now limited to the search bar and the sometimes frustrating display of search results. Building on the notion of recording consciousness developed by musicologist Albin Zak to describe the adaptation of musicians' playing styles to recording devices,[4] I suggest the term "algorithm consciousness" to describe the now common exercise of users adapting their search and listening practices to the "behavior" of ranking systems. Whether users adopt a "laissez-faire" approach or engage in this kind of game, "recommendations" are still presented as the ultimate answer to the paradox of choice (which can be seen as a theoretical fiction in itself), a problem that YouTube, as an online archive, has created for itself. In any case, it has come to dominate the available choices for distributing music on the platform. While presented as a consumer-facing offering, recommendations still serve a strategic need for the company and its other clients—advertisers. By encouraging users to get distracted by offers selected to maximize viewing time and session length (and doubling down on a relative initial prevalence, in YouTube consumption, of videos of far-right speeches or background music), while at the same time re-qualifying their activities in terms of choice and curiosity, YouTube can then package more effectively users' availability, involvement, and autonomy for advertisers. Here again, music seems to be crucial in the construction of YouTube's strategy as a company and as a "content" platform.

Playlists, Trends, and Mixes

In 2010, YouTube devoted a music section to a selection of concerts and "hits of the day," before giving music a more prominent place. Editors went so far as to place a "Music" tab in the middle of the home page in 2014. For a long time, music was the only category of production to benefit from this status, ahead of humor or video games, which have since been invested in heavily. A very clear insight into this growth of YouTube's music ambitions could be read in a November 2014 blog post:

You didn't just watch "All About That Bass" over 200 million times on YouTube. You watched Megan Trainor sing it live for the very first time with Jimmy Fallon and The Roots. You've used the song in tens of thousands of your videos as a cover with real bass. Your views helped push the song to the top of the Billboard Hot 100 for weeks. And it's all about one song.[5]

Much of this musical transformation of the site also occurred through the "Playlist" page, which actually followed the format of a national chart (Top 100 Music Tracks, US). Both the playlist and the charts are essential elements of the media that structure the music market. Their inclusion allowed YouTube to establish its position vis-à-vis a variety of actors: record companies, stores, radio, and traditional trade press such as *Billboard* magazine.

In doing so, the company was able to bring video viewing closer to the choice of listening to a radio station or buying a record. YouTube could be recognized as a place where musical popularity is measured actively. On February 21, 2013, AJ Frank, Head of New Market Development at YouTube, announced the integration of the site's US statistics into the Billboard charts:

> We have partnered with Billboard and Nielsen to include our U.S. data in their "Hit" charts - the Hot 100, Hot Country Songs, Hot R&B/Hip-Hop Songs, Rap Songs, Hot Latin Songs, Hot Rock Songs and Dance/Electronic Songs list. That is, all official YouTube videos, including user-generated clips that use licensed audio, will be factored into how a song's popularity is determined.[6]

The inclusion of statistics was an important step towards YouTube being recognized as a music medium in its own right, alongside radio and records. Despite blending in with these other media formats, YouTube still has its own unique characteristics. YouTube's music charts differ from those offered by magazine publications such as *Billboard* in that they do not display periodicity markers. Ever since sites like Last.fm and Hype Machine adopted the Audioscrobbler software, the principle of publicly announcing listening habits in supposedly "real time" had become part of Internet users' routines.[7] Building on their efforts, YouTube constructed its own temporality, which was neither their high frequency of updates nor the regular temporality of a print periodical.

The absence of a periodicity indicator, the number of "views," and the date of publication on the YouTube music charts suggested a hypothesis that has since been confirmed by a white paper written by YouTube engineers: on YouTube, success and freshness are combined to form something like velocity, i.e. the ability of videos to circulate at high speed; the videos that stand out according to this initial index are then re-integrated into the recommendations displayed on home pages and thus percolate up the broader charts. In this way speed becomes a self-reinforcing index that builds visibility. While in a traditional chart it is the mediatization of statistics by professionals and the general public (reached through various methods) that reinforces the successes in the making, here the ability to generate a large number of clicks in a limited time interval serves as a criterion of exposure, favoring an exponential logic.

Early on, the YouTube teams decided to reinforce this newer role of video ranking by promoting a specific "set of tools," YouTube Trends:

> YouTube Trends features new algorithmically generated feeds that highlight which topics and videos are trending right now. The site also offers a "top videos" module and a blog with in-depth explorations of videos, trends, news, and cultural phenomena seen across YouTube. We've also created a Trend Control Panel that lets you quickly explore what's popular in different cities in the U.S. and around the world, as well as within specific demographic groups.[8]

YouTube was not content to simply integrate its statistics into *Billboard*'s chart. The company competed directly with the magazine in the field of music consumption statistics, offering its own tool for monitoring the media popularity of music in the making. After the launch of Google Trend Lab in 2006 and the appearance of the Twitter Trends tool in 2008, YouTube Trends activated the proposal to represent "what generates the most activity, at a given time, within a given group of users."[9] YouTube thus became part of a movement in favor of an "algorithmic culture" on the Web, which not only describes the project of subjecting culture to the calculation of audience data, but also of valuing these operations as such and presenting them as a mediation worthy of special interest.

This shift in the form of legitimate musical mediation deserves to be highlighted. While to a certain extent music bloggers inherited the logic of the "flaneur," the "market observer" who, according to Walter Benjamin, has a kind of "occult science of the conjuncture," the reader of YouTube Trends was granted the power of a supervisor with new equipment for market observation, and invited to take an analytical (or playful) look at a statistical modeling of the social life of music. Reading YouTube Trends meant supervising the exponential; at the same time, the extreme granularity of the data attached to the number of views was reduced to a hierarchical order indexed on relatively banal socio-demographic determinations: gender, age groups, country. This level of detail in the indexes, which is higher than the kind of results communicated by *Billboard*, reinforces the idea that it is primarily on YouTube that a musical success is built "trace by trace" before any other media would register the aggregated result. YouTube thus performs a role that aims to capture what has been hitherto *Billboard*'s leadership on the reading—and ultimately the shaping—of what counts and matters in music markets.

In parallel with this rewriting of the market, YouTube has been changing its view of how site visitors consume music on video. Initially, "recommendations" were created as a response to the problem of "cadence,"[10] or the frequency of visits to the home page. Since 2015, YouTube has been promoting a new strategic goal, "stickiness" (retention) and has developed a specific tool, YouTube Mix, to achieve it.

Retention corresponds to the ability of a site to prolong a visit or, in this case, a "session" of consultation and viewing by the same Internet user. The criterion of frequency of visits is then secondary to that of "time spent" on the website. The importance of retention connects to a specific metric for video consumption, "Watch Time", which has replaced click-trough rates as a key factor in video ranking for recommandations (see p. 60). On a broad level, this metric is close to the principles of attention capture implied by the economies of radio and television, and to the framework of the attention economy in advertising; but in YouTube's strategy and discourse, it also encapsulates an idea of receptivity. This idea was articulated clearly in the company's public discourses. As T. Jay Fowler, head of music product development at YouTube, told *The Verge* magazine after the release of a mobile app, YouTube Red:

> A lot of people think of YouTube as a place where you come to consume, that you actively check out [lean forward], before you go elsewhere, but we want people to go there to lean back.[11]

As we have seen, "discovery" meant conflating relationships with the interface and with videos, and equating experience with consumption. The metric of Watch Time no longer sought to emphasize the management of channel subscriptions or to organize the choice between recommended videos, but to lead users to a more radical "laissez-faire." As with every new claim, this one did not replace the previous ones, but rather became a new focus in YouTube discourse and design. This promise of lean-back was embodied more specifically in YouTube Mix, a tool consisting of a continuous program of videos and advertisements linked together as users automatically drifted from one video to the next. This streaming playlist tool was in fact based on several previous experiments that had remained under the radar until then. Among them were thematic playlists related to contextual consumption, such as Gymnastics—years before Spotify bet on this axis of its strategy, claiming to be in the industry space of "Moments."[12] Following the same logic, and on the heels of a partnership driven by the majors (Vevo), came the integration on the site of full album playlist formats, characterized by their original cover and strict, coherent labeling.

The most important feature in terms of the shift in YouTube strategy, however, was the little-known YouTube Disco, YouTube mix predecessor. Its goal was to "automatically generate curated playlists of specific artists." Like many other YouTube tests, it was quickly discontinued, only to be resumed and transformed into distinct "mix" features (the continuous programming as a feature at any point through a toggle button; and the ability to launch a set/playlists of videos organized around a specific artist). YouTube team discontinued it with a touch of humor, but their explanation had a dark undertone that highlighted the overweening importance of strategic thinking: "We learned a lot from Disco, the results of which you can now see in the YouTube search engine and features like YouTube Mix. But like disco itself, the days of experimentation are over."[13]

Ultimately, the charts (at this point usually called "playlists"), monitoring tools ("Trends"), and automatic continuous playlists ("Mix") drew on the economics of radio and television, but also on the commodity form applied to music in the broadest sense, defining a specific cultural imaginary for YouTube's relationship to music and to the music listeners who use YouTube. In this period, always trying to find the right combination between addressing the "you" of the pseudo-universal and the "you" of the pseudo-singular, between the staggering presentation of an offer of heterogeneous videos and their supposed personalization in the recommendations, YouTube made a wide range of design choices. Each projected different attitudes among its audience, from the attentive monitoring of salient points in YouTube Trends to the laissez-faire of YouTube Mix.

The initial promise of facilitating discovery soon diffracted into multiple technologies, criteria of value, and ways of combining them. The mediation of music through musical genres, trends, or popularity indexes seemed overdetermined by strategies articulated around the performance and seduction of YouTube itself (from "cadence" to "retention"). They clearly stemmed from the desire to adapt YouTube to a competitive universe, particularly the emerging music streaming sector, and to enhance ideas of consumption and media exposure to satisfy advertisers. But it was more than a response to market forces, as they brought forward their own vision of what YouTube and music on YouTube could be: YouTube was now extending and rewriting, in its own way, the whole range of historical relationships between music media and advertising markets, from the excitement of musical fads elevated by television charts to the "leanback" listening of radio.

5

The Streamlining of Expression (2014–18)

While YouTube provided the music consumer with music videos and the music expert with charts, the company did not forget its early promises of enabling video expression and promoting the work of Internet users as producers, videographers, and channel editors. YouTube made a similar effort to streamline related activities at different levels, including a series of partnerships with major corporations and other older players in the cultural industries, discourses invoking "creativity," and tools to guide and coach users in their promotional efforts. Together, they encouraged musicians to adopt an entrepreneurial ethos, to manage promotion individually, and to follow new work habits. In this way, YouTube aimed to streamline music promotion by establishing routines for managing YouTube "channels." Of course, attempts to rationalize music promotion and distribution had existed before YouTube, but on this platform they took on a new meaning, according to its own norms, based on conformity to the role of the "one-man musician/entrepreneur/ community manager," with productivity and self-management as core values. Musicians, especially performers, were invited to adopt proto-professional standards of conduct, partly modeled on the site's other contributors ("creators"), and thus to think of the publication of their music in terms of successes or failures for which they would be held accountable.

The Televisionization of YouTube

YouTube has never stopped expanding on its initial promises to Internet users about the distribution of "personal videos." In 2007, the company introduced video ads (In Video Ads, August 2007). Later, it added a revenue sharing system with the most invested users (Partner Program, May 2007). In 2009, YouTube signed a deal with three of the four major record labels to provide regular music videos and programming (Vevo, December 2009) through a network of dedicated channels. These carefully crafted channels were marked by a logo that acted as a seal on thumbnails and as an official stamp in channel names, shifting the earlier focus on amateur aesthetics.

Vevo is said to have come about when Doug Morris, then head of Sony, noticed that YouTube was placing ads alongside music videos that were part of its catalog. This led him to rethink the status of the video as an advertising format and to negotiate with YouTube to make it a source of remuneration through advertising revenue. The Vevo project fed this ambition: it presented itself as a video syndication service with a collection of 45,000 videos, some dating back to the 1970s. These videos were republished through channels associated with artists and labels. Those channels also allowed their parent companies to display professional video quality in order to better attract advertisers, as the latter preferred to avoid "having their ads appear alongside low-quality local video content,"[1] while obtaining privileged rates on YouTube revenue sharing.[2]

These developments were accompanied by the hiring of cultural industry figures such as Robert Kyncl, formerly VP of Content Acquisitions at Netflix. Kyncl joined the YouTube team in 2012 specifically to develop partnerships with media and production companies.[3] The success of these initiatives, which saw YouTube go "downstream" in the value chain to fund a few shows and series, varied over the years, but YouTube never reached a point of credibility as a media producer in its own right. In fact, the first series of YouTube Originals have now completely disappeared from the site. On the other hand, such initiatives were a clear sign that the company was no longer interested in catering primarily to casual videographers, but instead wanted to reach all kinds of people and organizations involved in online distribution strategies, including the music industry, TV networks, and brands. As it moved in this direction, YouTube began to play at least three different—sometimes conflicting—roles: helping anonymous people succeed, serving as a promotional relay for major media or cultural industries, and acting as an ideal advertising medium.

Creativity as Watchword

By attempting to become as popular as possible on as many fronts as possible, and to connect forms and disciplines, YouTube was already seeking the broadest available set of ambitions. Since 2014, this dynamic has crystallized around the buzzword "creativity." The company's PR discourse affirmed YouTube as a bearer of ambitions and responsibilities. It extended the search for consensus beyond the various artistic worlds, neutralizing the existing tensions between large media corporations, small organizations like independent labels, and individual contributors or users. At stake in the "creativity" discourse was not only the minimization of differences between different actors and parties, but also the defense of an economic project and cultural policy that applied to, among other things, music, while at the same time reclassifying the Internet users who publish on YouTube as a pool of talent ready to be economically valued. To use a term from popular music studies, YouTube seemed determined to build its own proto-market.[4] This project involved a series of tools, documents, and speeches that normalized an attitude toward the strategic management of artistic expression. In the process, YouTube assumed the status of a "supermanager," defining the best practices of a musical sphere made up of artist-entrepreneurs.

The reference to creativity made it possible for YouTube to address everyone in the same way, and to gather the destinies of its partners and audiences around supposedly common objectives. In this respect, *creativity* was taking over the references to DIY, popularity or success, with music being now considered a form of "content creation" like any other. Yet, going back a few years, it appears that the reference to creativity on the platform had a more precise meaning, precisely in relation to music. Indeed, in a YouTube blog post entitled "Music that hits the right note" (November 2014), the "creativity of the YouTube community" specifically referred to users who were on the fringes of the professional music world. In this post, YouTube's music team updated the anthropological meaning of the word by referring to all the activities that involved "remixing, inventing, parodying, and doing a little bit of anything" to everyone's "favorite songs." More specifically, "Creativity" then referred to the work of contributors sampling more established artists in their own videos.

(One could argue that this accommodation had already been the reason why a site like MySpace was so attractive. MySpace had exalted the "contact" between "groups" and "fans" through the articulation of "subscriptions," "friends," "profiles," and messaging features. On YouTube, with the absence of a direct messaging tool, this contact took, for a time, the form of a feature called Video Responses, discontinued for good in 2013 and then limited to the videos comments).

YouTube's reference to creativity initially served to give coherence to what was happening on the site, allowing the company to assert its specificity while taking advantage of semantics that seemed to exclude no one. Beginning in 2012, publishers who created "channels"—YouTube's term for what are actually video listings that correspond to a user account—were renamed "creators" and became the recipients of guides, advanced tutorials, and specialized blogs that encouraged them to optimize their practices.[5] At the same time, however, the term has also been used in very different contexts, including major business conferences, to indicate YouTube's desire to develop "exclusive content".[6] "Creativity" could have been seen as a poor candidate to assert YouTube's singularity in the market, since the term was already widely used by a variety of organizations, especially through the rhetoric of "creative industries," which had allowed the UK government of the time to rebrand the nation as a leader of a new type of economy at the international level.[7] Yet few tech companies invested in the term with the same intensity as YouTube, which sought to transform itself from a challenger to the entertainment industry to a market leader, reassuring advertisers about the "safety" of its content and investors about future advertising revenues. YouTube's desire to appear closer to established production companies and TV channels was already evident in 2008, in the "pro-establishment" conclusion of a previously quoted presentation by Chad Hurley at MIPCOM:

> We are not today in the age of YouTube. Nor are we in the age of digital content or the age of multiplatform. The space we're in today is an extension of the work you all have done, it was built on the shoulders of CBS, RCA and other innovators who came before us. There is no such thing as old media. There is no such thing as new media. There is only one media with a common purpose: to inform, move and inspire the world through information, art

and entertainment. Together, we can find a solution that will benefit everyone in this ecosystem, from consumers or advertisers to content owners.[8]

In that speech, Chad Hurley insisted that YouTube was indeed a major media company like any other; however, other officials, on later occasions, continued to downplay YouTube's status as a major media company. For example, in 2013, at a conference for music professionals on the topic of music videos, Candice Morrissey, director of music partnerships, insisted that YouTube was only a "technological platform" and not a media company.[9] In fact, the company has always had to deal with its various audiences and partners by shifting its stance when necessary. Sometimes it presented itself as a simple tool via which aspiring videographers and musicians could expand their access to the public, sometimes as an accomplice to the efforts of large conglomerates to maintain their power; sometimes merely as the publisher of a tool whose reach depended on its user base; and sometimes as a media company in its own right with its own programming ambitions. Over the years, however, these fluctuating positions became fraught with real tensions: on the one hand, the goal was to allow the maximum number of videos to be published in order to uphold the "broadcast yourself" mission and libertarian notions of self-expression; on the other hand, copyright enforcement became increasingly impossible to avoid.

YouTube's regular design changes and shifting mission statements have partially circumvented these tensions. The technical, graphic, and strategic redesigns of the site meant that, to the general public and to journalists not yet accustomed to GAFAM's critique, YouTube rarely seemed to have the robust quality of a defined media company; and in the financial world in which Google (not yet rebranded as Alphabet) operated, tech companies were still a providential outlet for excess capital; turning assets into revenue-generating products, especially in the advertising market, seemed like a long-term game. Nevertheless, and despite the universal reference to "you" and the standardized nature of the tools and formats offered by YouTube, the company had to win over its various audiences and partners by making its various strategic positions fit together.

This meant neutralizing their differences through a common metaphor, played out for all and at all scales. On September 18, 2014, a post titled

"Investing in creativity" was published on the YouTube blog, this time signed by Alex Carloss, then head of YouTube Originals.[10] This speech dispensed with some of the rhetoric of complicity that was usually used on the official blog. It listed a litany of strategic actions in an objective and emphatic style that made it part of the exercise of institutional communication. The speech was a way of defending a now dominant position by adopting an attitude of ethical responsibility and offering an investment program to finance exclusive "content." This corporate story was about YouTube explaining and claiming its position as a patron, which until then had remained rather implicit. (In fact, it can be argued that by offering YouTube as a free tool for storing and publishing videos online—even if it did so by reconfiguring a certain amount of common knowledge and non-proprietary technologies—the company put itself in a position of authority over the future actions of the people using it, a position that the user license made explicit with a temporary license on all videos, its right to delete anything, and the prohibition for its users to modify the software, among other things). Perhaps for the first time, the text linked YouTube's position of authority to the mission of democratizing culture, no longer as a marketing claim but as a philanthropic mission statement. Creativity thus became the normative horizon of a private cultural policy in which YouTube intended to take a proactive line.

In this text, too, "creative" practices, although not precisely defined, were to be supported in order to satisfy fans. In a way, this scenario looked like the transposition into the private sector of the (now classic, especially in Europe) discourse of state support for the development of cultural/creative industries.[11] YouTube gave Internet users the tools to play the game of competition and to enter the market of media visibility, an operation that was supposed to benefit everyone: the company, the novice and professional publishers ("creators"), as well as the viewers and listeners ("fans"). This general discourse hid the arbitrations that such a project required. In fact, this scenario would have meant to reconcile the accompaniment of self-produced musicians towards professionalization and the strengthening of the means of promotion and remuneration of established artists. That said, supporting "young" creators by providing them with recording space might seem rather paltry compensation for the imbalance resulting from the promotional capacities of the major labels when it comes to promotion and marketing.

To be coherent, such a position requires that online visibility be organized by niches and strata, and that the curating function exerted by YouTube would favor no one—an idea that can exploit the opacity of the calculations of "recommendations" to establish itself. (Sociological research on online visibility has rarely found a leveling-up of visibility inequalities, but rather a strengthening of the blockbuster logic. Moreover, looking at the trajectories of both emerging and well-known artists discovered on YouTube, such as Justin Bieber, it is easy to see that these trajectories often required continuous effort over several years and relied on well-established professional intermediaries.)[12] Whatever YouTube's status in relation to these outcomes, the reference to creativity allowed the company to erase the issue of unequal access to media and public presence. It suggested a continuum of creative practices that shared the same goals and require more or less the same resources.

On another level, YouTube's use of "creativity" as a framework was also linked to a specific notion of cultural value. A technical conception of creativity, which can be found in the French word "ingéniosité," describes the simple proposal of an original solution created from pre-existing elements. This can be applied to forms such as mash-ups, which may be surprising in their own way, but remain essentially defined by a clever arrangement of known and recognizable elements. In contrast to this notion of novelty is aesthetic novelty. Of course, ideas of aesthetic newness are the bedrock of modernism in the arts, and they undoubtedly count as many definitions as there are historical regimes redefined by artists and critics—including, but not limited to, the notion of a radical split with the past attached to the avant-garde. Indeed, even modernist newness does not exclude forms of combining bits and pieces, as in Brion Gysin and William S. Burroughs' literary technique of *cut-up*. But it generally accepts them on the condition that they entail a reworking of and intervention around expectations in the perception, interpretation, and evaluation from which these forms derive their value. In this regard, even productions of (commercial) popular culture and popular music have been read by enthusiasts and critics to be part of the modernist agenda for cultural change,[13] or at least to offer pleasures that, despite industry constraints, are not entirely reducible to the mere satisfaction of a demand for a standardized set of parameters.[14]

Although in the past YouTube regularly ascribed special merit to particular artists and contributors through contests and ceremonies (see Chapter 3), this more recent discourse on creativity tended to suspend any kind of evaluative criteria for what might be important and valuable in video or musical practices. By conflating novelty and newness, YouTube's strategic mobilization of creativity equated an openness to everyone and everything, regardless of the qualities or specificities of what they do. However, this inclusive discourse about "creativity" should not be confused with an egalitarian vision of talent or an open-ended conception of aesthetics: rather, it meant that everyone who worked and contributed to the platform "created value," i.e., that every meaning, experience, or "use value" had a potential exchange value. Anyone who publishes on a YouTube channel is contributing to an emerging market, is an asset to themselves and to the company: this is the underlying meaning of "creativity" in this context. This means that any practice that is playful, a form of leisure, recreation or open-ended experimentation, can always potentially become good business, or contribute to the business of the company that hosts it. We have now become familiar with this logic of thinking, which is shared by most so-called "content creators" and "creative platforms," but I would like to emphasize that at that specific moment in time, this was not yet an obvious use of this vocabulary, nor a commonplace way of thinking about what it means to use online servers and video publishing tools. One need only recall the full range of competing discourses about what kind of mediation and social value YouTube was offering at the time: service, digital archive, social media, social network, user-generated content platform, etc. were all candidates for framing what is now seen simply as a "platform" for "content creators" who should never miss the opportunity to "monetize." In a way, YouTube was a step ahead of its apparent post-Marxist opponents who criticized the non-recognition of the "digital labor" coming from (at least some) platform users, as the company decided early on to view a large part (though not all) of the contributions made on the platform through the prism of their economic externalities. In any case, by focusing on the discourse of creativity, YouTube not only presented an ambition to become an institutional force and a series of investment projects to accommodate strengthened partnerships with the cultural industries. By embracing the full range of its meaning, the company also united all the clashing audiences and stakeholders that could be addressed as "you" and enrolled them in a project in which every expressive endeavor was to be considered from the perspective of its economic potential.

Learning to Self-Manage

Other aspects of the creativity speech were worth noting. Alex Carloss also downplayed the company's market power by emphasizing how creativity is a matter of learning, experimenting, and making mistakes, and how YouTube teams share an "adventure" with "creators." Using the lexical field of risk, uncertainty, and self-transformation, he seemed to bring YouTube closer to an experience of creation defined by its unpredictability. Uncertainty, however, takes on different connotations depending on whether one looks at it from an individual point of view—that of the experience of the creation process—or from a corporate point of view. The first instance is a psychological experience; the second is a managerial and financial issue that is a fundamental characteristic of the cultural economy, as a field where every strategy, from vertical integration to catalog licensing, is a response to the unpredictability of demand. Moreover, in this case, YouTube's risk-taking was limited by its decision to prioritize the funding of producers of videos that had already proven their economic potential ("we've decided to fund new content from some of our top creators"). Finally, Carloss did not say whether what he meant by "risk" refered to potential aesthetic failure (because of the poor quality of the programs) or commercial failure (because of the low audience numbers), or even if the company had the will to distinguish between the two. In any case, his statement normalized the connection between uncertainty and success, as if risk was a necessary evil; moreover, risk was valued implicitly for facilitating the separation of the talented or deserving from the rest. In this context, the uncertainty of cultural/aesthetic value was confused with a way of experiencing work and management that was by no means specific to cultural/aesthetic expressions: entrepreneurship, the organization of work through freelance, independent, short-term contracts, and more generally the precariousness associated with the individualization of professional paths. This implicit link between experimentation and entrepreneurship assumed that the market was the ultimate and rightful judge of what makes creation valuable, but also that there was no difference between creation as an uncertain process and project management as risk management.

In fact, this idea of risk control as a necessary and important part of creation was one of the reasons used to justify a new aspect of YouTube as a tool to organize, monitor, and continuously adjust the marketing and promotion of videos and music. "Creativity" can be seen from a third angle and takes on a new meaning when it is translated into the status of "creators." Here, the creativity discourse no longer plays out as a way to bridge between the site's audience and the company's partners, or to encourage the people who publish on YouTube to see themselves as valuable content creators; being a creator means implementing strategic thinking to publish and promote videos, being entrepreneurial, and sharing the company's bold attitude.

Through its many guides and tutorials, YouTube set the standard for professionalism, performance, and productivity. The Creator Academy (now replaced by an official YouTube channel called YouTube creators) was a training tool for everyone, including musicians (in case that was not clear enough, the page features a DJ). Its rhetoric conveyed all the trappings of institutional legitimacy and offered step-by-step advice for anyone learning how to properly edit and program a "channel." Here, YouTube was following a path already familiar to its parent company. According to Thomas Grignon, Google's pedagogical rhetoric had allowed the company to "present itself not as a company serving private interests, but as an actor involved in the transmission of knowledge and the professional integration of its students." Grignon summed up the orientation of the Creator Academy as follows:

> Although the user can access numerous and varied data, it is a search for volume largely inherited from audiovisual media audience measurement that still seems to prevail today. Number of views, average time spent on a site, number of subscribers, likes, shares or comments . . . are progressively becoming the spontaneous way of understanding published content. For

Google, these criteria are the sign of good "performance" of productions. And the values displayed on the user's dashboard, of course, are intended to be perpetually increased. A video will be "performing" if it obtains results in line with or higher than those measured during the previous publication. It is not enough to measure effectiveness; we must constantly work to optimize it. It will be necessary to work to reduce zapping and criticism, to increase the number of views, shares or citations that are still insufficient ... Led to project themselves in a perspective of progress, the user is his own reference[15]

The individualization of trajectories and practices of self-evaluation thus passed through hyper-formalized procedural knowledge based on the language of authority. These discourses could thus make us forget their very general character, in relation to the desire to provide a model that applies to everyone ("solutions for all"). Seeing standardized procedures may be surprising when you think about the early days of YouTube. It is less so, however, if one recognizes the fact that distribution and communication practices in the music industry have already been formalized, be it through training courses or music marketing manuals.

The Creator Academy encouraged channel editors, through recommendations, to pay attention to the design of their pages and the layout of their videos in order to make them unique and cohesive. It also encouraged them to publish on a regular basis videos that were formatted according to criteria that were believed to capture the attention of Internet users. In these unsigned recommendations, YouTube gave a definition of the videos' *mediagenie* on the site, an ideal format for the "YouTube video." After promoting novelty effects (albeit relative) in its early selections, YouTube now promoted rules closer to the rhetoric of early vlogs.[16] In this framework, musicians were encouraged to become channel managers and to act like music marketing specialists by applying optimization approaches to themselves and their relationship with their audience. Such advice constructed an (implicit but ubiquitous) syllogism according to which good use of the available tools was almost enough to achieve success. The material conditions of making music were thus reinterpreted: they became less conditions to be dealt with as best one can—by finding different ways to support and sustain a creative practice, by achieving autonomy in the plurality of interdependencies[17]—and more a new priority to be achieved as quickly as possible: that is, to win in the battle for attention.

At the same time, YouTube can reap the benefits associated with making explicit and objectifying what was sometimes experienced as a dangerous implicit in the relationship between artists and labels: its deontological and dialogical rhetoric could be perceived as an expression of a form of justice that aims to level the playing field in order to give everyone an equal chance to prove themselves in the marketplace. Such a prospect may have seemed appealing as a way to move away from the paternalism that was and still is common in the industry. For example, when Charles Cadras, the head of a collective of independent labels, was asked about their possible extinction, he replied: "It's great to give a group $500,000 to make a video, but who is going to negotiate with the singer when he takes too much LSD or when the number of streams collapses?"[18] In contrast to such discourses, YouTube's seeming technical neutrality, while claiming that musicians were taking back control of their destiny, could be appealing, but it also replaced the clichés of the bohemian lifestyle with another artistic stereotype: the figure of the musician-entrepreneur endowed with an impeccable work ethic.

The idea that the trials and tribulations of creation–the doubt, the adventure, the openness to the unexpected—could be replaced by regulated know-how and the adoption of standardized tools can seem reassuring. According to this idea, it would be enough to do what YouTube suggested in YouTube for Creators in order to benefit from the roles of professional videographer, channel programmer, press agent, or market researcher. However, this model of empowerment places the burden of work and responsibility—when the results are different from what was expected—on the isolated individual[19] and encourages tendencies toward self-evaluation, which in turn leads to the privatization of anxiety.[20] In this model, numerical indicators are the right criteria for revealing or verifying talent, as a result of the demand they are supposed to represent, relegating all other criteria to the sidelines.

With the emphasis on view counts, it has become more difficult than ever to distinguish between what is the result of the aesthetic quality of a particular song/video, one's (in)competence in community management and strategic thinking, and one's talent or one's fame. As Jeremy Wade Morris has shown, the optimization of both publishing and musical practices has become a new standard as algorithmic ranking systems orient listening.[21] Much has been written about the right "recipes" for YouTube success, and this book is more concerned with the broader logics that link music and media technologies than with deciphering soon-to-be-obsolete ranking models. In the case of YouTube, depending on the time and place, optimizing could mean, among other things, publishing videos on the same channel at a regular pace, favoring productions located at the intersection of several semantic chains, presenting aesthetics compatible with relaxed consumption, using the right thumbnails, keywords as tags, and even "cheating" (a turn of phrase that would imply that algorithmic visibility is a game, not a structurally unequal system), by exploiting various loopholes, for example by resorting to new forms of payola.[22]

In this context, and contrary to frequent reports of this or that "YouTube success," the success of a piece of music or a video is not a matter of popularity as such (if it ever could be), but also depends on one's personal capacity to take into account these specific conditions and to act accordingly. Finally, the existence of direct interventions to game the system, or the difficulty of translating the success achieved on YouTube into other spaces, such as critical acclaim or the sale of recordings or concert tickets,[23] are all ways of putting into perspective the YouTube discourse that equates success with the adoption of the right ethos and good "creator" practices.

From 2015, as music became a priority on the site, YouTube began offering more specific advice to musicians through a peripheral site called YouTube for Artists (it still exists as of the writing of this book). This satellite featured a series of videos in which many established artists (Ok Go, Robert Delong, Suroosh Alvi, Action Bronson, Alexa Goddard, Lindsey Stirling, YP, Nicki Minaj, and Tinashe) were enlisted as exemplary consumers of the tools and tips offered by YouTube. In these videos, which work very much like testimonials, their success is used as an incentive. The videos are edited in such a way as to make very short speeches particularly coherent, both at the level of one artist and from one artist to another. They offer a kind of exquisite corpse of the typical soundbites about disintermediation: "there's been a big break between 'today' and '20 years ago';" "Pandora's box is open, the world is ready to hear anything;" "there are more opportunities for an emerging artist than ever before, so it's up to the artist to be the pioneer who leads the way;" "you have to make sure you take advantage of every opportunity to make a name for yourself and build your audience;" "today the Internet gives you your own record label;" "you don't need anyone but yourself to make things happen."

Although YouTube is never mentioned by name, the fact that the brand implicitly presents these statements suggests that its tools are a necessary step in achieving the success embodied by the artists who speak. These artists are essentially performers (singers, rappers, musicians), but what is really valued in these videos is their multiple skills and multitasking abilities. The short films alternate between backstage scenes in which the artists talk about their self-promotional practices and scenes of interaction with an obviously captivated audience. These videos serve as a transition to YouTube's more specific instructions, which encourage the reader to take care of the fans.[24] This injunction updates the classic tendency to base artistic autonomy on the direct support of an audience that has an affective attachment to one's music, for new tools such as "fan funding" buttons; this familiar theme, however, when it comes to the experience of star artists, and which usually takes into account the constraints that come with it (to the point that at the time of writing, music media are reporting how some artists are now refusing to play into the "toxic attachment of fans"), is here unequivocally advocated for unknown or emerging artists.[25] Of course, by this time the idea of the audience as the primary source of artistic autonomy had already been largely reintegrated into the thinking of music marketing consultants and managers under the label of "direct-to-fan" strategies.[26] There has also been a shift by some music companies away from the business model of a record label to that of an artist services agency, all well beyond the limited perimeter of YouTube activities. Change is a constant in the music industries. Nevertheless, YouTube had a specific role in normalizing the promises of disintermediation by choosing to speak to the artist as a (presumed) individual, inviting him or her to engage in the work of the community manager, the advertising strategist, the audience analyst, etc.

All of these different roles have been presented as corresponding to simple operations, although in practice they are all potentially new and time-consuming tasks. Moreover, they depend on cognitive and affective knowledge, since they require one to project oneself into an empathic relationship with the public while simultaneously assuming a position of strategic oversight.[27] This is a form of emotional labor[28] in itself: the aspiring artist must force admiration by cultivating a professional artist's ethos and, in a double bind, constantly operate in two roles at the same time.

The ability of artists to embody and display, through media, emotions and an identity that could be confused with the full range of their experience and existence has often been presented as a key to success and a valuable criterion in popular music and popular music studies. This ability has implications that are aesthetic (expressiveness), affective (spontaneity), moral (sincerity), and communal (authenticity). From an analytical point of view, it is important to be able to differentiate all these dimensions, which are at play in both musical and promotional practices: for example, aesthetic appreciation means recognizing a know-how in performance (just as the taste for emotions in reality shows does not require believing in the reality of situations), while moral appreciation implies a latent critique of the division of labor and heteronomy of musical practices in a market system, as well as a conception of self-sovereignty.

In this regard, it is important to note that despite the normativity of these guides and tutorials, YouTube does not seem to explicitly exclude genres or scenes a priori. But it is clear that the focus on emotions and self-identity in music and its promotion is accompanied by exclusions. The "ideal YouTube musician" participates in genres or music scenes in which the individual musician/band and his or her relationship to the public, the ideal of an abundance of intersubjective, meaningful, almost Habermasian communication through music, seems to be in the foreground; pushed to the margins of this normative ideal are numerous other possibilities that are just as valuable, such as the sharing of sensitive experiences, the collective transformation of musical expectations, or the experimentation with ways of life,[29] from punk hardcore to niche online remix cultures, from club cultures to improvised music scenes. This doesn't mean, of course, that traces of these cultures and productions have no place on YouTube's servers, but rather that they are implicitly made contingent in what the corporate discourse defines as its overall project, and risk being rendered "less efficient" in terms of the norms that suit YouTube channel management.

If the call to present oneself as caring has a specific potential on YouTube, it is because it presupposes that the musician-entrepreneur-manager is no longer responsible only for her work or her performances, but also for an audience with which she is supposed to enter into a mediated/intimate relationship. This relationship, translated elsewhere as audience engagement,[30] evokes the reclassification of brands' online communication strategies as a *conversation*.[31] This vague reference to a dialogical relationship, by evacuating a good part of the implicit rules of face-to-face interactions, has allowed brands' communication to be reclassified in order to adapt to the supposedly new spirit of social networks without upsetting their rather strict mechanisms. To return to YouTube, musicians have been asked to create intimacy and contact by asking questions of the audience, writing comments in response to each message as quickly as possible, and keeping an eye on statistics to choose their topics. They were told not to hesitate to add "hearts" or "likes," to use voting forms, or to produce unscripted videos: a whole range of skills and objectives is to be implemented systematically, making one wonder what links them to a supposed "intimacy." Musicians who followed these instructions would then be able to turn the site into a space for gathering and capturing commodity audiences, for themselves as well as for YouTube: it has been up to the musicians to seduce people and gather them into a commodity audience,[32] and then up to YouTube to use these musicians' output to sell advertising spaces to brands.

Through these discourses and tools, did YouTube enable the end of the division between creative and promotional work, giving musicians more autonomy? Or has it normalized an ethos and activities that risk changing the culture of creation (if it can ever be detached from mediatization)? In any case, by putting forward the ideas of "creativity" and the democratization of the means of publication and promotion, the company pretended to give users the means to emerge from a competition that it both stimulates and regulates (as it does with Vevo). YouTube presented itself as the best choice to achieve autonomy, while reconfiguring it around relatively strict "good practices" in its protocols, as well as its own aesthetic and ethical standards. In order to reinforce its business model, the company positioned itself on a ridge between the invitation to bypass the music industry and the call for artists to adopt its constraints by embracing multitasking, responsiveness, productivity, reliability, and investing fully in the work of promotion. These were all ways for musicians to show that they were professional enough to seduce the YouTube teams that recruited their "Partners". This meta-management of music, a strategy of orienting Internet musicians towards an attitude that was itself strategic, also allowed YouTube to guarantee the conformity of the videos with the expectations of the brands. In principle, "creativity" worked to appeal to different audiences and cover multiple ways of being a musician and being productive on YouTube, but as we've seen, it easily slipped from valuing everyone's originality to orienting its musician audience toward self-management and hard work.

6

The Hit Machine Narrative (2012–18)

If, as we have seen in the previous chapter, YouTube has taken steps toward building its credibility in the field of artist promotion, its success also depends in part on its ability to hold up as examples those who have achieved their success "thanks to YouTube." In October 2013, the French newspaper *Le Monde* ran the headline "YouTube, machine à tubes" ("YouTube, Hit Machine").[1] The industrial and mechanical metaphor has worked as hyperbole since Theodor Adorno's early work on popular music. The point in this article, however, was not to present YouTube as a new "cultural industry" in its own right, shaping the public's tastes, but rather as an ideal space for musicians in search of fame: "In the United States, the video platform has become the number one source of music listening for young people, and new artists owe everything to it. It's reshuffling the deck in the music industry. YouTube has become 'the place to be for anyone trying to reach a young audience.'"

In the article, the portrayal of YouTube as an opportunity is essentially based on an analogy with mainstream radio channels. The site is described has having replaced the large, hard-to-reach channels in the record companies marketing strategies. What is not said, however, is how these same record companies manage to make their videos stand out. The reported remarks of Laurent Bonneau, head of rap and R&B radio Skyrock, focus on how he consults YouTube in order to gauge the popularity of already-released songs, rather than to discover new ones. The rest of the article does not try to assess the role of YouTube in the success of the artists mentioned, even if the main claim is that their music appeared on YouTube for the first time, that they found their first audience there, that they were discovered there by major record companies (Irma Pany), or that it offered them opportunities to differentiate themselves thanks to the promotion of their videos (Woodkid).

The exaltation of the dominant role of the "hit machine" was reconciled, without concern for contradiction, with the comments of other intermediaries, such as the talent contest site MyMajorCompany or the label Green United Music, who described the place of YouTube in their own strategies: it seems that other actors had to come and invest their own work, like so much coins in the vending machine, to trigger success. The relationship between musical success and YouTube is a trope based on an implicit syllogism: because music is present on YouTube, it is the site that has determined the fate of artists, and what has happened to them is inextricably linked to its potential as a medium.

This *Le Monde* article is just a more general example of the treatment offered by the press to the success of a list of artists ranging from the pop singer Justin Bieber (discovered when he was a teenager) to the South Korean rapper Psy, via the trap-rap producer Baauer or live electronics musician Madeon, crystallizing the formula "YouTube phenomenon."[2] Released in July 2012, Psy's video for his song "Gagnam Style" set a new record for YouTube statistics. It then served as a benchmark for the press, even though it was the press itself that turned the video into a "YouTube phenomenon" that was supposed to represent how music was evolving in contact with a new tool and distribution space. The video shares many of the characteristics of other successful music videos discussed earlier (see Chapter 2), including the choreography of an "unruly body" and the emphasis on the exoticism of a stereotypical setting. In a persistent echo of Matt Harding's early exploits, the choreography, the variety of settings and situations, and their potential to elicit new variations seem to be as important as the song. According to Psy, YouTube was crucial to the success of his song. In particular, YouTube allowing for for derivative videos and remixes was seen as the decisive feature that allowed his song to become wildly popular. In any case, the press used this hit to highlight a new paradigm according to which parodies and covers by Internet users would have a significant impact on the success of a song. Rather than being a break with the model, Psy's video is actually a moment of crystallization of these strategies for promoting covers and remixes: Madonna launched her Dance On business in 2011 to offer brands the potential of choreographed covers on YouTube to communicate with customers.[3] In 2013, the rapper Soulja Boy had success with a video featuring choreography that already looked like a parody (of Superman moves).[4]

The fact that the "popular success" of certain artists and songs is regularly attributed to the power of YouTube is part of the company's PR. In a blog post entitled "A YouTube built just for music," product manager T. Jay Fowler offered a perfect example of this: "Usher discovers Bieber. Psy breaks a billion. Macklemore goes from the garage to the Grammys. Pentatonix top the charts. Over the past ten years, music on YouTube has been magic. We've seen established artists reach new heights and new artists explode on the scene. We've seen our fans shake, get happy and let it go. And together, they've made YouTube the absolute best place in the world to discover new music."[5]

These discourses lead us not so much to want to propose an explanation of how a specific song has become a "YouTube success", but to nuance and more precisely delineate the role of YouTube by isolating it among a series of factors, and to understand the recomposition of the multiple mediations that constitute a musical success. It is therefore a question of interpreting rather than explaining the movement by which values are invested in music, in its appropriation by the public, its media formats, and its accompanying narratives.

Taking this perspective, rather than trying to compare incommensurate phenomena, we should take into account the fact that each success presented as "viral" is also presented as one-of-a-kind, and choose a specific song to analyze in more depth the process that such vocabulary (virality, YouTube success) tends to obfuscate. Of course, the risk is that the proposed observations lack generality, but it is also the condition for drawing the thread of a series of mediations that are likely to illuminate other situations.

I will proceed by trying to reconstitute, from a first release on YouTube, a chronological course of online events and documents, each one outlining what is at stake (the video of an important encounter, a sound file to comment upon, a song to critically evaluate, a hit to revel in, a specific story, etc.) and preparing for further requalifications/interpretations. This approach is inspired by what Catherine Saouter called the "semiotic pathway" in an article that also studied a YouTube video, and addressed questions of cultural legitimacy.[6] I propose to transpose this notion to the way music moves online in order to understand how, far from only "providing access" to music or transmitting information about it, each media format (the Soundcloud waveform as much as a piece of journalism or a graph) brings its values and meanings into play.

At the time of writing, a number of articles in the specialist press and the YouTube Trends blog were focusing on the song "Alaska" by the singer Maggie Rogers, who had been unknown prior to that. What is interesting from our perspective of how music changed YouTube is that, as we will see, this song was one instance (among the several we have already mentioned) where YouTube boldly and explicitly decided to position itself as the "hit machine" that *Le Monde* described. In fact, if we recognize the importance of this narrative, we can say that music not only changed YouTube and helped define it, but also "made" YouTube: it helped build its reputation as a place where artists and musicians go to build their profiles, meaning that in return, their presence attracted more and more people.

"Alaska" did not enjoy unprecedented success, but it was still significant for a first song: it reached thirteenth and eighteenth place on the charts in the "Adult Alternative" and "Hot Rock Song" categories respectively in *Billboard* magazine. As of January 15, 2018, it had accumulated more than eleven million views on YouTube in its two main versions. "Alaska" first appeared in the form of a demo played at a masterclass at New York University (NYU) attended by the prolific composer, producer, and singer Pharrell Williams. A video of this session was then posted on the artist's YouTube channel "IAmOther," discussed by Internet users, especially on Reddit, before being covered by the specialist music press, which included the video of the masterclass in their comments. Maggie Rogers eventually posted a new YouTube video for "Alaska" that is more like a traditional music video.[7] She then credited Debay Sound, a label that hosts only her own productions, and which is licensed to Capitol, a label owned by the major Universal.

When Reaction Precedes Listening

The first video is already loaded with symbolic stakes. The conditions of possibility of identifying a "talent" are played out simultaneously on three levels: NYU is already a place of selection through "merit;" Pharrell Williams assumes the role of "talent detector;" and the video's presence on YouTube makes it a candidate for the forms of classification and visibility offered by the site. Pharrell Williams, as an invited judge, assumes some of the authority of the academic institution. At the same time, through his presence and curiosity, he draws attention to the video and the song it features, thereby distinguishing it from all the others circulating on YouTube. The young singer who performs her song is actually auditioning three times at once, in different ways: first, as part of her curriculum at NYU; second, with Williams as artistic director; and third, when IamOther publishes the video, to Internet users. Insofar as each video is associated with comments and view-counters that prepare the appreciation/encounter of/relationship with the music, each listening on YouTube is also a special form of audition. Everyone is able to verify the adequacy between what they are listening to and the public success: the number of views and plebiscitary signs such as the like would testify to this.

In the video, when Pharrell Williams hears the song, he rolls his eyes, almost sheds a tear, and is left speechless. He turns his gaze to the young woman, as if trying to reconcile what he hears with who she is. The producer films this in a single shot, partly reminiscent of the style of TV talent shows, from the exaggererated facial expressions of the *American Idol* judges to the dramatization of the acousmatic relationship between voice and performer in *The Voice*. The scene in which the young woman appears visibly intimidated is also part of a gendered configuration well known in the world of popular music, where a male producer seems to have the power to make the career of a female performer, even though in this case Maggie Rogers is also presented as the composer and performer of the song. While at first glance the video shows the direct affective reaction of one of the song's first listeners, it also has a mediagenic dimension.

This mediagenic effect is redoubled for Internet users who discover the scene in video on YouTube. Literary theorist Sianne Ngai has described the contemporary meaning of vulnerability as an aesthetic or para-aesthetic value, as crystallized in the adjective "cute." She has also shown that "excessive reactions" have become an object of cultural appreciation in their own right, involving an affective and sensitive relationship to the world that differs from traditional aesthetic categories, as illustrated by the famous "double rainbow" video, which shows a man stunned by the sight of this optical phenomenon.[8] The many reaction videos that show the expressions of children and teenagers as they open presents or hear a song for the first time, then create an environment conducive to receiving the affected faces of Maggie Rogers and Pharrell Williams. At the same time, this video took on added significance because it did not follow other characteristics typical of videos produced for YouTube. Because it was a scene shot in a particular situation (in this case a university), and not addressed directly to a possible audience of Internet users, the video was valuable as an objective testimony of an unexpected event captured by the camera. In this respect, it was similar to the style of videos in which an unexpected gesture or a rare phenomenon occurs—one does not expect to see such emotional responses in a university setting. Given that Pharrell Williams is a celebrity and has to maintain his conventional image in traditional television appearances, this singularity of the scene is reinforced and it offers a moment of rare intimacy. By paying attention to the form of the video and its mediatization, we can see how the qualities of such an unusual moment of video are added to those of the song in order to frame its reception.

Once published on YouTube, the video was accompanied by comments from Internet users. They offered different ways of interacting with the scene, the image, and the song. These appropriations ranged from minimal embodiments of taste judgements, to more performative speech expressions ("this song was dope"), to exercises in style that expressed affective engagement in viewing the scene. This is the case of the Internet user "upotheke" (March 30, 2017),[9] who reacts to Pharrell Williams' speechlessness by imagining the inner monologue he might be having.

On May 25, 2016, the video was posted on the Reddit forum under a new title. This one, in turn, insisted on the star's emotional response: "Such a genuine reaction from Pharrell to an amazing song (skip to 18:15)." Half of the comments on this page focused on these ethical rather than aesthetic dimensions: it was less about evaluating a video than about discussing the ethos of the protagonists, i.e. the modesty Pharrell Williams seems to show and the vulnerability of Maggie Rogers: "It was incredible, you could see how nervous she looked;" "Man, if I had to play him my music, I'd be so uncomfortable."[10]

About Vibes and Soars

If the statistics provided by the YouTube Trends blog are any indication, the feature of Reddit's video edit on online music magazines significantly increased its number of views. But at this point, it is no longer the same object that is perceived and discussed: the "revelation" of the song to Pharrell Williams visible in the video and its affective implications for Internet users become an element of context. The song thus becomes doubly autonomous. It is disarticulated from the source video to become a sound file, notably on the music online blog/magazine *Pigeons & Planes*; and it is transformed into an iconic waveform and thus an autonomous musical entity, on the Soundcloud platform.

This autonomization of "Alaska" as a musical recording (rather a mix of a song and a media "moment") also happened through the way different journalists talked about it as a "pop song." *Pigeons & Planes*, in an impressionistic style common to music blogs, spins a climatic metaphor that seems inspired by the geographical reference of the title: "In Maggie Rogers' Alaska, the clouds part, the sun rises, and the blinds of a dark room give way to light."[11] The *Los Angeles Times* builds on this geographical perspective: "Maggie Rogers grew up playing the banjo in rural Maryland, then slowly came to appreciate dance music. This commitment is a little unusual, but if it produces music like this, I'm all for it."[12]

Pigeons & Planes also features an interview in which Maggie Rogers emphasizes the psychic states she wants to translate through music ("the meditative dimension I reach while climbing or dancing"). *Slate* picks up on the passages that most emphasize the "crafted" dimensions of her concept: "A lot of the rhythm of the song started when I tapped a beat on my jeans. That sample is the main rhythm. It's me snapping my fingers in a room."[13] The insistence on the rural experience, a favorite theme of a "folk" mythology in the music industry, is easily reconciled with the profile of an ingenuous and reserved young woman with inherent talent, which does not prevent her from being reflective and capable of articulating her ambitions, things that are expected of the student that she is: "I wanted to make dance music or pop music sound as human as possible" (*ibid.*).

Pigeons & Planes builds on this reference to musical genres to pivot the perception of the song. The song is then defined by its formal structure, this time inscribed in a certain type of pop music. The description recalls a musical figure common to the period, referred to as the soar, a kind of rise that runs through the song and recalls the power ballads of contemporary singers such as Lorde: "What sounds like a soft-spoken soul begins to soar, liberated, as the record progresses."[14] *Vulture* magazine, for its part, embraces a reading by musical genre, focusing on the mix of "electronic," "pop," and "folk,"[15] while the *Los Angeles Times* reporter reinscribes the song in a wider trend of hit songs: "I won't deny that this song reminds me of 'Royals,' but that's probably just because of the catchy hook."

The song is successively reconstructed as a mediator of emotional tone and mood, as an example of the universality of music as a form of communication, as an expression of a country girl's authenticity, and as a combination of generic and stylistic conventions. Critics synthesize authenticity and spontaneity (rooted in geography and psychology) with artifice (a generic and stylistic construction). The critic's sensibility and predilections thus redraw the contours of the song each time.

The Prototypical Story of a Song's Success

At the end of June, *Pitchfork*, the leading magazine for the indie rock/pop scene, broke with these heterogeneous perspectives by taking an original stance. By proposing an animated GIF of Pharrell Williams' surprised and admiring expression, the magazine testified to and legitimized the interest of certain groups of Internet users in the original video and the song, but also in the way it provoked a strong emotional response even from an experienced producer well used to analytical listening. At the same time, it reinscribed "Alaska" into the structure of a relatively conventional narrative around the figure of an aspiring and promising artist who must transform hype into success.[16]

The *Pitchfork* article mentions for the first time, but does not elaborate on, a co-producer named Doug Schardt. His profile on the recruiting site LinkedIn reveals that he worked as a music supervisor at VIACOM, MTV's parent company.[17] Although the article focuses on the aesthetics of the song, it no longer describes it as just another news, but instead as a media phenomenon that deserves its own story, as evidenced by its presence in a section called "The Pitch". The question is whether Rogers will be able to follow a destiny that seems to be the only one that deserves interest: that of a popular, commercial, and lasting success. The title puts the magazine in the position of referee. Pharrell Williams' video has created a musical and media phenomenon, the durability of which must now be measured: "Pharrell's stunned face launched Maggie Rogers' career. Now what?" Here, the song is no longer confused with the reaction of Pharrell Williams or Internet users, but it is not entirely autonomous in its effects: it is now the narrative of its media circulations that precedes and frames it.

On July 8, 2016, the YouTube Trends blog spotted the way "Alaska." was being noticed in the media. An anonymous author published a post titled "How musician Maggie Rogers ended up with a viral hit on YouTube"[18]: "In the last two weeks, 'Alaska' by Maggie Rogers has been one of the most dazzling successes on the Internet: in just twenty days, it has amassed millions of streams across the web." The rest of the post shows a statistical curve. It depicts a very low curve, the passage through Reddit, and a spike at the time of the features by *Pitchfork* and *USA Today*. Even taking into account the video's being retitled on Reddit, the chain of appropriations and symbolic reconfigurations is thus mainly reduced to a trajectory of influence that builds a cumulative success. The graph indirectly suggests a kind of step-by-step transmission, close to the principles of Paul Lazarsfeld's two-step flow of communication and its consequences in so-called word-of-mouth marketing. The graph connotes scientific notation; here it suggests the possibility of making comparisons between "contents" in order to increase generality and identify rules of "virality." The biological metaphor of virality used by the site is based on more recent theories of diffusion, but it suffers from the same difficulties as these theories of two-step flow. This notion is accompanied by an indifference to the variety of forms and predilections involved in the processes of mediatization: musical, expressive, and communicative meanings are replaced by the model of the transmission of a cell or a biological entity, whose chances of contagion could be measured independently of the interpretive capacities of individuals, groups, their experiences and the particular and dynamic social situations in which they are inscribed. "Virality," especially when it is associated with a quantitative notation rather than with a description of symbolic qualities and stakes, in fact proposes a simplified vision of these processes, dividing them into a schematic division between a "potential" internal to the object and a favorable "context."

The studies that focus on this paradigm reveal the difficulties of identifying and weighing autonomous factors among complex and situated cultural productions. The temporal coincidence between the media that have become points of passage and the increase in the curve is not enough to prove that these media are the cause of the increase in diffusion. While the YouTube Trends blog offers a picture of social and statistical trajectories, its ambition is not to understand the conditions of an aesthetic consensus. The post is based on a rhetoric of observation, presenting and reconstituting the song's trajectory as an objective and more or less linear phenomenon that passes through a series of points, rather than attempting to question its conditions of possibility. At the same time, by emphasizing the idea of a viral hit in relation to this curve, it maintains the confusion between the simple publication of the video by the user in a shareable format—the YouTube player—and the effectiveness of the site as a distributor or promotional agent. This syllogism is reinforced by the image of the graph that depicts the evolution of YouTube views. The post also reads: "Alaska's success inspires many covers, remixes and tutorials on YouTube."

YouTube's name overhangs the success curve and appears at the end. If such a post then allows the site to keep its promise of revealing creativity, it does so by shifting YouTube from a listing space to a partial cause of success. The piece does not distinguish between the provision of resources to edit and brand videos, the distribution and promotion methods present on the site, and the activity of the audience. The company thus presents its own image of what constitutes the media circulation of a song as a non-linear but formalizable trajectory of success. The site poses as an objective observer in order to emphasize its own power.

Tracing the circulation of a song like "Alaska" allows us to take a step back from the media narratives, whether carried by YouTube or by newspapers and magazines, that make the site an active auxiliary of emerging talents and their success. Despite the specificity of the initial situation of listening to a song at NYU in the presence of a star, it reveals the variety of mediations that contribute to the construction of a song's meanings and potential. These appear in the successive re-editions of the video, which has become a song to be listened to on specialized media, itself constantly redefined as a more or less singular musical form, as part of a narrative about the revelation of a new talent, or even about the contribution of YouTube to the manufacture of success. Each of the spaces in which the value of the song is constructed potentially carries the temptation to explain its success: by the power of the guest's brand (Pharrell Williams); by the use of sites and forums to transmit a sensibility, affects, ethics that filter the attention to the music; by the power of prescription of the specialist press; or still that of YouTube as a source of emerging talents. In regard to this complexity, we can understand how it might be tempting to reject the weighting of these "external" factors of success, to prefer to explain it by the musical strengths of the song itself, or to take the side of skepticism, focusing on the classic scenario attributing agency to the powerful male co-producer behind the scenes, who already works at MTV.

The various discourses constantly oscillate between the will to justify the collective interest in the song by its intrinsic qualities (as in the generic and stylistic criticism of the music media), to describe its cultural or media conditions (as in the *Pitchfork* article), or to reduce it to the influence of one or more media. But it is only by bypassing the decomposition between "internal" and "external" factors of success that we can grasp the more subtle issues of *mediagenie*, woven into a narrative that crosses the various forms in which the "selection" of talent, the ranking of videos, the sharing of affects, and the promotion of "content" are interpolated.

In this way, we can observe cross-distributions of the legitimacy to qualify music. Music criticism and YouTube, each in their own way, unravel and renew these complex relationships, where it becomes clear that the videographic and musical object is never given in advance and never remains quite the same. The substance and identity of the document is modified, and the narrative about the relationship between forms, media, and audience is recomposed each time.

Even if it is difficult to follow the discourse of the blog YouTube Trends when it suggests that YouTube is a crucial cause of the song's success, one can still detect a certain logic in this recomposition. It is in line with the tendency of record companies and institutional cultural mediators to expect artists to prove themselves to an online audience first, referring to these early signs of popularity in the justification of their own choices. Although highlighted by YouTube, the rather specific case of Maggie Rogers, a young NYU-trained artist now working with the Matador label, clearly deviates from the model of the independent artist's creativity and unmediated work that the site otherwise values. But it shows that despite its integrative and totalizing discourses and devices, YouTube does not play all the roles in promoting the artist and constructing her success, and its share of responsibility is far from being determined. The process of a song's mediatization is complex: the definition of a song and its boundaries as a form are stabilized according to media apparatuses and social commentaries that constantly re-map what belongs to music "itself" and what is "the noise" around it. The social construction of musical success is never the result of the work of a single entity, if only because artistic directors, music critics and journalists, data analysts, and, of course, scholars like myself all compete to prove their expertise in the public sphere. Yet, when mainstream and legacy media celebrate YouTube's success, they tend not to mention the strategic work of individuals and companies that aim to generate replays and "virality" of videos from the outset.

The description of YouTube, by the company itself and by other media, as a "hit machine" risks confusing what is related to the tastes of Internet users, what is related to the successful match of the original video with YouTube-specific ranking parameters and display formats (the video image, the choreography, the humor, the premium on interaction that allows certain songs to reach different audiences and cross-classification categories), and finally YouTube's more general influence (either on a symbolic or a purely statistical level) on the music market (charts, etc.). The company is thus building itself as a quasi-institutional force at the heart of musical culture, independent of any reflexivity on the cultural and aesthetic significance of these musicians or the specific relationship that Internet users have with them.

If YouTube presents itself as a discoverer of artists, facilitating the circulation and massive appropriation of their songs, elsewhere these hits are never quite reduced to a position in a ranking. The valorization of a "hit machine" works only if the songs seem to aesthetically resolve the paradox between the different notions of success as massive circulation directed from above and the organic selection of songs from below. But most stories about YouTube as a "hit machine" do not seem to consider it necessary to contrast what should be ascribed to the public's taste or to YouTube's influence in the creation of hits. The mediatized public and the medium itself then become one and the same. Theorizing the relationship between YouTube and musical success in this way excludes both the qualities of the music and the autonomy of the audience, while reducing the process of mediatization to a reductive equation: presence on YouTube = chances of popularity.

7

(Semi-)Automating Authorship (2007–18)

After promoting music as a major theme on its home page, YouTube's new strategic direction in music seemed complete when, in 2015, it launched a new commercial offering dedicated to music, allowing internet users to consume its rich catalog of music tracks (official versions and alternative videos combined) for a fee, without having to endure ads: YouTube Music Key. After an initial commercial failure, the service was relaunched a few years later as a mobile application, YouTube Music. But in order to allow access to works without a priori filtering, YouTube had to give guarantees to publishers and record companies. These guarantees became a tool with the evocative name of Content ID. This tool appears to be a simple management tool and semi-automatic application of copyright, but it actually changes its scope and underlying philosophy: authorship becomes less grounded in a qualitative assessment of aesthetic value, always available for revision and debate, and more a projected feature of musical works "themselves" as combinations of data, reachable through probabilistic calculations.

The Origins of (Semi-)Automatic Copyright Control

The management of copyright by YouTube is based on a multiplicity of spaces, moments, and documents that participate in the creation and maintenance of a legal regulatory framework for the circulation of music. To understand this process, one must read the strategic and promotional speeches published by members of the site's team, legal texts, legal reports, records of judgments, and finally the patents and technical documentation of tools and algorithms.

From the outset, Content ID addresses YouTube's need to maintain its status as a host while assuming the control functions of publishers. This system goes further, however, in that it privatizes the application of copyright rules under the aegis of a single company and extends those rules to practices and forms of music or sound that were previously partially exempt from those rules. While the system claims to reduce the difficulties of control, it actually changes the way it works, placing the record companies in charge of semi-automated procedures. Computer models produce a positivist objectification of an ontology of sound, of perception, of the singularity and originality of works. They establish the difference between original and "derivative" works, or define the value of the use of previous material, a process that in this case is removed from public deliberation.

We have already noted that YouTube's position on the presence of copyrighted video and music has been unclear for several years. While a strategy memo from Sequoia Capital, the investment fund that acquired YouTube in 2006, summarized the company's plan around the category of "personal" videos, according to consultant Mark Mulligan, the company entered into financial agreements with the majors that same year, presumably to avoid litigation. In some respects, the Web was initially conducive to experimentation with distribution models, but when it came to music, many of the start-ups trying to develop listening devices or online music-shopping sites failed to secure agreements with rights-holders and were forced to close. In this situation, the qualification of listening devices from a technical and media point of view played an important role. The categories of "listening on demand" or "Web radio" have thus led to various agreements with the record industry. This kind of qualification mainly concerns the status of companies and sites as hosts or publishers, and through these conditions, the way in which they can or cannot protect themselves from copyright infringement.

This distinction is critical to the attitudes of music and audiovisual industry lobbies, governments, and the judiciary toward Web sites. Depending on which option is chosen, websites can appear as threats or as partners. In fact, different types of rights are at stake, in particular the right to copy or the right to broadcast. In his study on the construction of the online music market, Jean-Samuel Beuscart notes the importance of defining media devices:

First of all, it is necessary to decide whether the Internet is more about reproduction, representation, or both; and, if there is reproduction, to prioritize between the different forms of reproduction: in particular, between durable inscriptions on the user's hard disk, and temporary inscriptions on the servers (caches) of access providers, hosters, or partial ones on users' hard disks in the case of streaming.[1]

The fate of a Web site depends not only on the agreement reached with rights-holders or on the power relations with public authorities, but also on the interpretation of its technical and media characteristics and of the applicable legal framework. Because the Web is structured as a network of servers and documents, definitions of "host" and "publisher" cover plural and often ambiguous realities. Legislators and legal authorities categorize them according to how sites define themselves on the surface, but also according to the identification of their underlying technologies. Thus, in 2007, the lawyers of the European Audiovisual Observatory considered that the ability to manipulate recordings in order to move them from one site to another via an embed code (see Chapter 1) was sufficient for YouTube to go beyond the status of a hosting service. YouTube's "Terms of Use" also establish a licensing agreement for the exploitation of works that would bring the company closer to the status of a media company (editor).

Every analysis in this book has come to the same conclusion, showing the extent of the site's activity in defining standards that visibly guide what is published, what is visible, and what is consulted. However, every lawsuit filed by cultural producers has resulted in YouTube being recognized as a hosting service.

In the United States, the rule for hosts is known as "notice and stay down": it requires the filtering of works after the fact. It was introduced by the World Intellectual Property Organization (WIPO) and implemented in the US in 1996 by the Digital Millennium Copyright Act (DMCA). This law limits the legal liability of online "services," then defined as "an entity that offers to transmit, route, or provide connections for online digital communications, between or among points specified by the user, of material subject to the user's selection, without altering the content of the material as sent or received." Through the obligation to designate "agents" to whom it is possible to address appeals to request the removal of controlled works, the WIPO, the DMCA, and the law for confidence in the digital economy in France ("Loi pour la confiance dans l'économie numérique"), have decided on a relatively tolerant framework for the designated services, removing their responsibility to host these works in the first place. These texts state that the hosting company is not a priori responsible for the presence of infringing documents on the site and that it must remove them only after explicit notification. This limited responsibility allows YouTube to escape a WIPO procedure called the "three-step test," which defines the conditions under which it is possible to recognize an exception to copyright. It is likely that it would be difficult for YouTube to pass this test, since it requires the company to prove that it does not have "the ability to act on the hosted content" and that it does not perform "acts of exploitation of the work."

The mechanism of the YouTube player has probably contributed to YouTube's ambivalent legal status. Because it seals the recording in a visible, recognizable format and marks it with the YouTube stamp, the player takes the recording beyond mere storage to a public manifestation of the marks of an editor's handiwork (in the sense of the editor who fixes and guarantees the material form of the "text"). It is through the player that YouTube maintains control over the circulation of what it stores and derives benefits from it, such as the collection of usage data. The YouTube-style player differs from other, earlier sites, such as those that collected multiple copyrighted sound files on a single page and in a single player, and relied on the power of links—the source files remained stored and hosted on Internet users' blogs. YouTube, on the other hand, blocks access to the source file by converting it into a stream. The file is never downloaded in its entirety to the user's computer, but rather passes through it "in dots," packets of data that are successively "read" before being deleted (see Chapter 1). In this way, YouTube appears to Internet users as a recording and listening device, while from a technological and legal point of view it prevents direct access to files more firmly than other hosts.

These considerations demonstrate the concern of publishers and record companies to control the distribution of works, a concern that is as old as these industries. In principle, their task is to maximize the financial benefits of the works that are fixed on media (these media participate precisely in anchoring the legal unity of the work-commodity). To do this, they have been able to rely on the collaborative projects of Internet users to identify the pieces of music circulating in MP3 i.e. large collective databases such as CDDB. Online music and video publishing tools intensify this strategic challenge and its political stakes: should the circulation of copyrighted material be controlled, and how? In a book titled *Copyright's Highway*, Stanford law professor Paul Goldstein uses the phrase "celestial jukebox" to link the charm of the old device with the utopias of the immaterial, to defend to media conglomerates the idea that "with a few tweaks to copyright law, they could monetize their catalog holdings in a promising new medium." Two American communication scholars, Patrick Buckart and Tom McCourt, described the crystallization of this concern in the combination of customer relationship management (CRM) and digital rights management (DRM) technologies:

> We argue that, despite its witty name, the Celestial Jukebox actually works in a way that desecrates online music sharing by using two discrete, but intertwined software applications—CRM, which is designed to address the 'right' content to the 'right' consumers at the right time in their online activities, and DRM, which is designed to prevent unauthorized copying of content and enforce restrictions on its use. When combined, these technologies provide a personalized online experience for consumers within the confines of what Strauss (1999) calls a 'Digital Fort Knox', an impenetrable fortress protecting a rich treasure. The recording industry requires a new infrastructure, both to protect the copying of unauthorized files shared on peer-to-peer networks, and to create an alternative to physical (brick and mortar) stores.[2]

YouTube's system for identifying protected "content" is in line with these ideas. But the advantage of the YouTube player, which combines the availability of video and sound with the inaccessibility of files, does not seem to be enough for the biggests cultural producers. After the acquisition of YouTube by Google in 2006, it was therefore "under pressure from the companies" that the identification system was introduced, initially as a video identification tool (Video ID). In fact, it comprises a set of microdevices and formats: a "content" tagging system; an organization of several documentary systems that make it possible to compare a video being uploaded with references registered in a database; a system for automatically blocking the upload and proposing substitutions; and screens that invite the rights-holders to apply a technical regulation, choosing between three options—allowing the Internet user to publish a video without compensation, monetizing it, or blocking it.

While watermarking had been around for a while, the principle of identifying media or computer resources was developed specifically for video and music by the Californian company Audible Magic. Founded in 1999 on the promise of "automatic content recognition" systems in the audio domain, the company benefited in 2000 from the acquisition of another company specializing in consulting and the sale of specialized software in this field, Muscle Fish LCC. It was then able to register a series of patents such as "a system for distributing decoy content in social networks," "a method and device for identifying a work received by a processing system," "copyright detection and a method and system for protection," or "a method and device for creating a unique sound signature."

The Audible Magic website now highlights an "automatic content recognition" solution. It claims to have developed the "de facto standard for identifying music to verify its legal compliance with content recorded by the majors and major music aggregators" and lists customers such as Facebook, Soundcloud, Twitch, or Vimeo. According to *Tech Crunch*, Audible Magic signed a licensing agreement with YouTube in 2006, shortly before competitor MySpace. The name Content ID used by YouTube appears to have been registered as a trademark by Audible Magic. The appropriation of this name was the subject of a dispute between the two companies, which would mean that the system proposed by YouTube for identifying videos was first developed with the inspiration, if not some of the resources, of what Audible Magic designed for music.

In 2007, YouTube tested its enhanced version under the name Content ID in partnership with Time Warner and Disney, but YouTube made it official in late 2008, with a focus on music, in a post titled "The ups and downs of music licensing on YouTube." The company made the audio and video ID system official by explicitly presenting it as a way to build a partnership with the music industry:

> We are working with the global music industry - the majors and independent labels and publishers, rights collection companies, and with artists and

songwriters directly - to produce user-friendly licensing agreements. With these partners and our cutting-edge Content ID technology, we have created a win-win situation of a kind never seen before: a system that gives artists completely new sources of compensation and a fantastic way to connect with their fans.[3]

Despite the rhetoric, Content ID did not work as a "win-win" deal from the start: the major Warner Music initially used it to block the use of music from its repertoire, before changing its tune and walking away from the deal with YouTube after the first year, citing insufficient profits. In 2009, YouTube filed its own patent for "blocking unlicensed audio content in a video hosting site," before regularly communicating about improvements to the system. A more thorough definition of the feature was finally presented to the public in April 2012:

Content ID allows rights-owners to automatically detect uploaded content that contains potentially infringing works. This is made possible by a system that creates a 'fingerprint' of a video at the time it is uploaded to YouTube. These fingerprints are automatically compared to references provided by partners. If there is a match, rights-owners can choose to monetize it, block it from the site or track viewing metrics. Because of the large scale at which YouTube operates [. . .], this is an automatic process.[4]

It seems clear that Content ID is a technical response to the "notice and stay down" recommendations, a response that, by automating the process, allows YouTube to more easily process all takedown requests from rights-holders. However, Content ID not only facilitates an existing procedure, but also reconfigures the philosophy of copyright and authors' rights, inviting us to rethink the way works circulate on the Web. Indeed, among the three possible options mentioned above—"allow" (and track metrics), "block," or "monetize"— monetization introduces something new: it invites rights-holders to track how works, or fragments of their works, circulate in order to keep them online and collect potential advertising revenue. For Hunter Walk, a YouTube product manager, this represents a decisive advance for online expression in terms of copyright. It encourages "creative manipulation" better than Wikipedia's contributory encyclopedia and Creative Commons free licenses ever could. According to Walk, YouTube "beats them" in terms of "scale and value" given the economics of music and video rights management. This perspective ignores the fact that the individuals and collectives behind these projects are not necessarily seeking to maximize the technical efficiency of copyright processing. Non-profit organizations such as Wikipedia or Creative Commons are primarily concerned with cultural and political change, hoping to intervene in the existing legal framework of copyright, to generate new practices of shared resource management, or to expand the domain of non-market activities. Later, Hunter Walk even acknowledges the limitations of Content ID from this perspective, with an implicit reference to the failure of global licensing and fair use extension projects:

> What YouTube has put in place is not a change in the copyright/fair use [framework]/DMCA process, but in fact a commercial relationship outside of those laws. Some might say it's far more important to change the law—because it applies to everyone—than to have wealthy companies building systems outside the legal structure.[5]

However, he immediately dismisses these questions in the name of the creative and profit-making opportunity that the system represents:

> Why do I love what YouTube has created? Because it allows tens of millions (hundreds of millions?) of videos to be enhanced by combining different pieces. Then because it's an elegant way of recognizing that content has commercial value and if you use someone else's, it deserves a return. And because it creates a new subversive base—a generation is growing up on the premise that it's okay to remix things.[6]

Hunter Walk's enthusiasm may be based on the idea that YouTube is reversing the general trend toward the gradual strengthening of copyright. YouTube can congratulate itself on having succeeded in opening up regimes of expression where the advocacy of global blanket licensing has failed. The post concludes with the liberal axiom that corporations are the best agents of change for the benefit of all:

> The biggest changes in copyright come not from the U.S. legal system, but from entrepreneurs, technologists, and capitalists who see it as an opportunity and a way to grow their market rather than fighting to share the same pie.[7]

This view of Content ID values the interdependence between the company, the "creators" and rights-holders, and the defenders of freedom of expression and creation who would have a vested interest in seeing "remixes" emerge from a gray area between tolerance and secrecy.

Selling Consensus

Despite its appearance as a technical solution and regulation of existing practices, Content ID involves a complex set of techniques and a redefinition of the culture of online music sharing. This process requires a special effort on the part of YouTube to gain the support of record companies as well as its users, who occasionally publish videos that are likely to be "detected." With regard to the revolution announced by Hunter Walk in a space reserved for specialists, YouTube's discourse aimed at its various audiences to explain how Content ID works and to enhance its potential took a seemingly less ideological turn. It was less a matter of extolling the ideological breakthrough achieved by the innovative company than of adopting a pedagogical rhetoric to familiarize them with a technical and social arrangement that should no longer be open to debate.

Content ID is presented in an animated film with attractive colors reminiscent of educational videos. The people involved are portrayed as stereotypical characters with loosely defined faces and specific needs. Each character, recognizable by typical details, performs one of the gestures configured by the new system: a man in a suit and tie chooses to "block" the video, someone in a colorful jacket with shaggy hair chooses to "let it go," while a third character, with a guitar slung over his shoulder, shakes wads of cash because, according to the voice-over commentary, "he's starting to make money with [Content ID]." This makes it clear that Content ID is all about music. The first protagonist seems to symbolize the executive of a large corporation historically concerned with controlling the distribution of media, the second the potential artistic director of an independent label, while the third is a rock musician always looking for financial opportunities.

Although Content ID first emerged under pressure from media conglomerates, the caricature of the man in the suit from the major label is interpreted here as a way to convince the "rebellious" musician to manage his own rights with Content ID without a record label. At the same time, rather than emphasizing the potential power struggle between artists and record labels, the video concludes that there is an ideal compromise between all of these types of music rights-holders and their audiences: "Artists can let fans reuse their content, and fans can create promotional and business opportunities for their favorite artists, making Content ID a true win-win for new forms of creativity and collaboration around the world."

In the film, the ID system is presented in the form of large random series of colored cubes that pass through a dizzying system of pipes and computers. The imaginary of the Fordist factory, in a literal reactivation of industrial culture, meets that of cybernetics through the dynamic management of the circulation of resources. Such a phantasmagoria of production and logistics obviously requires the smoothing out of all the nuances inherent to the digital processing and the formatting applied to the recordings. The graphic vocabulary thus combines representations of the management of culture that are both distinct and coherent: a total commensurability of works, as well as of behaviors, and a full intelligibility of calculations, as well as the ideal of a dynamic balance between actors within the system.

These harmless images appear to be a way of assuming, while de-dramatizing, the project of an industrialization of culture based on the application of an ideal of governance to copyright. Alain Supiot defines governance as the extension of the principles of the scientific organization of work to parts of society that are not part of industry.[8] The film shows the importance of inscribing rules in systems of management and control, and of applying the well-understood interests of rights-holders. It reduces the specific situations in which music and law are interpreted to a pseudo-casuistry in which each actor acts punctually on an individual level and in a predictable way. What could be seen as the pedagogical necessity of generalization thus reveals at the same time the conditions for the system to be consensual and efficient.

All of these conditions suggest an ideal of law as a system that tends toward perfect social regulation, bypassing its inscription in a history and in a space of conflicting interpretations. Such a vision of law is very close to the ideal of the scientific organization of work around automated tasks, followed by its evolution towards the perspective of self-regulated and optimal man-machine systems: for Norbert Wiener, the ideal of legal predictability is already a good model for cybernetic theory, "in the sense that it deals with problems of regular and repeatable control of certain critical situations."

Taking seriously the images proposed by YouTube then allows us to take into account the affinity between law and technology that underlies the technical and organizational operationalization of copyright. At the most concrete level, Content ID is indeed based on a technical process that involves the creation of a database of identifiers for pieces of music, the automatic processing of sound and visual material, and a series of enforcement and control operations thanks to the cooperation of the actors who own or manage music rights—be they labels, publishers, distributors, or musicians.

An Industry of Variants

Such a procedural and technical operationalization of the law operates according to the symbolic and political stakes of copyright. In principle, copyright raises a number of political and ethical questions. Does borrowing or sampling come at a cost to the creator? How do we arbitrate between fair compensation for artists and the right of access to culture? What use of previous material should be allowed or prohibited, and under what conditions? What should be in the public domain rather than on the market? How to determine, on a case-by-case basis or according to general rules, what should prevail between the public's right of access to culture and freedom of expression, on the one hand, and the right of publishers and authors to control access to their works or to be remunerated, on the other?

These questions are partly answered in the spaces of public deliberation—laws and jurisprudence—or in the details of synchronization agreements in which publishers, labels, and musicians assess and negotiate the value of using a piece of music as a soundtrack. These agreements often ignore a whole range of (re-)uses that touch on the moral rights of the owners of the works, but are a priori without commercial intent. Traditionally, rights-holders have not always sought to control unofficial remixes, bootlegs, reproductions of unpublished works (live recordings, demos or studio recordings), parodies, educational quotations, or even very short musical fragments in documentaries.

In principle, the three options offered by YouTube (authorize, block, monetize) leave room for all scenarios, since they include the possibility for publishers or producers to authorize all productions. In this way, Content ID has made it possible for songs from back catalogs that are not widely played to exist online and to generate profits, even if they are very small. By relying on the moral philosophy of copyright, they allow it to be applied systematically and beyond current habits on the Web. In fact, the very existence of the form changes the implications of the laissez-faire choice, by leading to the application of rules by default, or by requiring an active approach to laissez-faire regulation.

The very conception of the tool, allowing control in a single click implies that not acting on one's copyright is equivalent to not recognizing oneself as an artist (in the case of a musician user) or, for an intermediary such as a label, to renouncing one's task as an editor. In a subtle way on the site, but blatant in the slogan "Copy–Remix–Profit" used by Hunter Walk, the system—by its very existence—transforms the status of what is identified and what is circulated to a potential commodity. This is what happens with videos, but also with all the marginal appropriations mentioned above: once the option of "monetizing" exists, why give it up?

With the "monetize" feature, Content ID draws a boundary equivalent to a private blanket license, a free zone where different types of reruns or uses of previous material are allowed as long as they are profitable. On the other hand, if rights-holders prefer the "block" feature, they are able to remove productions that do not suit them, even if they fall under exceptions to copyright that are provided for and tolerated outside of YouTube (for example, parodies or short samples). At the discretion of YouTube's back office, rights-holders are free to exclude any derivative production of their works.

Moreover, given the importance that YouTube places on the expectations of advertisers in recruiting "partner" users, forms with subversive potential are likely to be subject to self-censorship or preemptive deletion, as is the case on Facebook. This leads some legal experts to speak of a "privatization of censorship".

Far from overturning the status quo, YouTube could be seen as a practical development and expansion of the tendency of copyright extension. By introducing a kind of mandatory royalty for the publication of identifiable pieces of music, Content ID participates in this movement to expand the sources of revenue associated with the exploitation of copyright. According to Vincent Bullich, although they often pretend to defend artists, the tendencies to extend copyright mean above all "the privatization of expression,"[9] "the shifting of the appropriation of works from authors to publishers," "the restriction of creative possibilities and uses," and "the increasingly pronounced subordination of what and how to communicate to economic demands." The argument based on the need for a fair remuneration of authors is questionable: for example, Pierre-Carl Langlais, on the basis of a study based on SACEM statistics, states that in France, both today and in the past, there is no correlation between the extension of the scope of copyright and the growth of artists' income.[10]

To get a sense of what the consolidation of legal and economic authority over music means, one only has to confront it with the discourse and images of the "digital magma"[11] associated with the circulation of poorly informed and poorly controlled MP3 files on the Web in the early 2000s (see Chapter 1). The culture of producing and sharing remixes or edits of music tracks moves from a semi-public and informal expression to an explicitly public character under the aegis of a single company. In the same way, the common denial of responsibility on certain YouTube channels that deliberately publish controlled tracks (via the disclaimer messages stating "removed upon request") is both clarified and rigidified.

YouTube teams are aware of the risks of overusing removal procedures, and have implemented an "appeal" or "claim" system. To address the limitations of Content ID, the company is moving away from automatically blocking detected videos and requiring action from rights-holders. It also offers new tools that allow publishers to predefine a default duration of approval or prohibition, while immediately anticipating the limits of this solution by standardizing a "representative range." As a result, YouTube requires rights-owners to closely monitor the results of automated copyright control:

To the extent that Content ID cannot identify context (such as "educational use" or "parody"), we give partners the tools to use duration and match share (match proposition) as a proxy. Of course, this is not a perfect system. That's why two videos—one of a baby dancing to a minute of a pop song, and another that uses the exact same audio clip in a university lecture on copyright recorded by a camera—can be treated identically by Content ID and removed by the rights owner, even though one may be fair use and the other not. Rights owners are the only ones in a position to know what is and is not allowed in the use of their content, and we need them to implement their policies in a way that is consistent with the law.[12]

To minimize the pitfalls of Content ID, YouTube, following a logic reminiscent of the cybernetic principle of adding control systems to probabilistic systems, added another management system—the "appeal process"—in October 2012:

Users still have the ability to dispute Content ID claims on their videos if they are convinced that the claims are invalid. Previously, if a content owner rejected this challenge, users had no recourse for certain types of Content ID claims (monetization claims). Based on feedback from our community, we are now introducing an appeal process that gives eligible users a new option in the event of a case where the challenge is rejected. When users submit an appeal, the content owner has two options: withdraw the claim or submit a formal DMCA notice.[13]

The appeal process is based on an order to the parties involved to take responsibility for the system malfunction. The automatic rule applies first, before the decision can be challenged in court. Only in the event of a complaint from the user who originally posted the infringing video, may YouTube ultimately refer the matter to the courts. It allows users who feel that their video has been unfairly blocked to request a review of the situation by the site's teams, but poses a few difficulties (latency, legal standing to file a complaint, etc.). This appeal system embodies the general spirit of the system, which consists in delegating the tracking and identification of pieces of music and their appropriation to an interpreting automaton. It puts human teams—those of YouTube, of the artists, of their representatives, or even of other commercial intermediaries who choose to specialize in this new task—in the position of controlling possible residual errors or borderline cases. Publishers, musicians, and labels then perform repetitive tasks in a semi-automated process. They can either choose to approve, reject, or monetize videos with a series of clicks, or they can define enforcement rules to make the process fully automatic and save themselves the effort.

Beyond these general principles, the reference to "millions of videos" and "combinations of content" in Hunter Walk's blog shows that the project is built primarily to trigger related rights from "fan culture" videos, such as mash-ups, covers, or parodies. YouTube integrates and reshapes the culture of appropriation and musical remix in a space where its own criteria of decency, interest, and authorship prevail. The company increases its capacity to singularize works and stimulate their diffusion. The identification of a document in relation to a source not only allows the legitimization of a unique "text" in order to better multiply and valorize its commercial reproductions: the attribution ("claim") via Content ID legitimizes a single origin that is at least partially idealized (an author function in the sense of Michel Foucault's understanding of the phrase).[14] This allows the multiplication of versions, rearrangements, excerpts, and duplications, which in turn become commodities. The device subtly discourages the exercising of moral rights in order to increase the rent coming from advertising and proposes to replace the control of musical formats and their distribution by profits from variants. This model may remind us of the time when publishers made money from the sale of their songwriters' output, even if they were recorded and released by other performers and competing labels. The difference now is that the ownership of the sound "itself" in the form of a re-coded frequency sample takes precedence over that of the composition of a melody or the writing of lyrics.

The identification system and the semi-automatic processing procedures, far from being an a priori consensus solution, restructure copyright management and raise new questions. With semi-automatic removal systems, the first "content" deposited in the reference database runs the risk of arbitrarily taking precedence over the second. The interests of the rights-holders who have placed their works in the database determine which expressions are authorized (or not) for all other users, i.e. those who are not working to have their productions recognized as works in their own right. In fact, access to the registration of works that can be searched for in the YouTube database is not equally open to all. In order to enter recordings into the YouTube database, one must subscribe to a set of eligibility conditions one must "own the exclusive rights to a substantial body of original material that is frequently uploaded by the YouTube user community" and then be manually "approved" by the YouTube teams.

If we look not only at the status that allows access to the deposit procedure, but also at the conditions that allow a production to become a "work" sanctioned by an identification code, we discover that "only works with exclusive rights can be deposited as references." Here, the term "exclusive" actually creates a second category of "sub-works;" in practice, any parts of these attributable to other authors would not have been the subject of a contractual transfer of rights procedure and they are therefore particularly at risk of disappearing or never appearing. This would include any song based on samples that are too recognizable, any work that uses interpolation (the practice of including an excerpt of lyrics or melodies from another work), any remastering of works whose original composition is in the public domain, or even any sound art, especially field recordings.

The terms of access to Content ID show how the "win-win" system advertised to Internet users is in fact designed to favor one category in particular—the category that was targeted from the start, namely media conglomerates like Warner, which have vast catalogs of duly authenticated productions. As a result, the model touted as an opportunity for "remix culture" is actually closer to a variant industry that gives a premium to actors who are easily recognizable as owners of rights, or even many rights ("a substantial body"). The larger music publishing companies (which may belong to the majors) and possibly the new commercial intermediaries (such as distributors specializing in "digital music" or companies aggregating YouTube channels, so-called multi-channel networks) are thus in a privileged position to offer Internet users a shortcut to access the benefits of Content ID. For users who post videos containing fragments of identified recordings, this means that a rights-holder can decide the fate of a video at any time.

On the other hand, for the Internet user who has used an identifiable piece of music, "monetization" is not much more desirable than "blocking," since the rights-holder captures the advertising revenue generated by his or her video.

Beyond the financial question, "monetization" has a symbolic aspect. An "authorization" via the semi-automatic system is not equivalent to the recognition of the status of a "derivative" or "transformative" work for the piece of music or video in question. Rather, it is a matter of profiting from it as an advertising medium without going through the recognition of any authorial input: in this paradigm, the musical or audiovisual "remixes" of "creative" Internet users are not considered as "creations" in their own right. The monetization by Content ID transforms them into stand-ins for the works managed by the music and media industries, even if they represent only a part of the video in question.

Rather than opening up "creativity" to all through the authorization option, YouTube establishes a kind of variants industry in which the site can act as co-publisher, authentication agent, and regulator of access to a rights market. Despite references to openness, creativity, and remix, the company establishes a division between official works and derivative productions. This double-trigger system distinguishes in the structuring of circulation and remuneration flows between official artists, who deserve to be remunerated, and more casual "fans," who are merely granted a new right to use the works of the former without being censored—a right that is in fact only the correlate of a hardening and arming of the control of these uses. A separation between first works and transformative uses, which is difficult to establish from an aesthetic, legal and technical point of view, is anchored by the device. The catalogs controlled by the rights-holders and deposited in their database have (temporarily) force of law.

8

Experience as Traffic (2016–18)

If the copyright identification system is the first step in reconstituting music as a commercial resource on YouTube, the second step is to "monetize" the videos that contain the songs by placing advertisements on them and calculating the rights-holders' revenue based on consumption. Since then, and in parallel with the introduction of advertising on YouTube in 2006, the view-counters associated with videos have been gradually transformed from what was essentially a way of ranking them for display to a market indicator capable of determining values and revenue streams. This counting of "views" involves a dense process of capture and transformation between multiple activities, inscriptions, and symbols. It brings together the amorphous links between numbers and success with the professional cultures of television, marketing, and computer science, and reactivates the work of representing what viewers, consumers, and Internet users "do" in order to construct heterogeneous flows of value. From view-counters to patent diagrams, a series of shifting words, figures, and indicators constitute the ridge between figures of evaluation and technical and economic systems. By pulling together the thread of the "view," we obtain an extended series of categories, values and formats that participate in the achieved density of the "view" as a connection to popularity and success, both seemingly inescapable and regularly contested. In this chapter, I will show how the "view" is constructed as a general equivalent, as a trace of consumption, as an operator of conversion that links music, video, and advertising, and as an indicator of trends. Because the view functions as a standard, it is contested in more ways than one: I will map these distinct types of critiques. Finally, I will ask what a "view" really indexes, and how it contradicts what the word itself suggests.

The View As General Equivalent

The "view" is a composite object par excellence: it is not quite a sign, a concept, or a practice. Instead, it is a bit of all three, holding together the relationships between documents, actors, and ideas in a series of situations. The multidimensionality of the "view" is shared with any type of audience measurement and is at the same time what it must deny by operating an "alignment of a whole set of objects and actors."[1] In fact, "views" are linked to a variety of social practices: listening to music, watching a video, measuring the composition of an audience, setting up an advertisement and determining its distribution costs, comparing statistical curves located in time and space with targeted advertising actions, or identifying the external sites that led to the video. The reference to the "view" coordinates these practices on the double level of inscriptions (the "data") and symbols (starting with the numbers) in order to organize the infrastructure of a market.[2]

The status of the "view" is supported by press articles, advertisements, record-company press releases, as well as ordinary conversations, but here I propose to understand it from the situations organized by YouTube to establish and negotiate its value, in databases, processing systems, and various screens. When the "view" is at the center of all attention, it in turn establishes a variety of relationships: between Internet users (in their "profiled" identity) and their practices, between advertisers and the results of their investments, and between musicians and their audiences. By creating chains of equivalence between a series of activities, it participates in the establishment of the market or supports its definition: it serves as a reference point in concrete situations of exchange (such as screens where there is a fee for broadcasting an advertisement) as well as in the abstract structure that makes the market a set of regular practices and a structure of competition. In this respect, the view functions like money, since it is both concrete and abstract, in turn "a unit of measurement, a means of payment, a standard of value or money of account, a reserve of value and, finally, a means of exchange."[3]

"Views" are in fact meant to transform practices into signs and signs into vectors of transactions on the advertising market (the "views" of videos increase the number of "views" of the ads associated with them and the value of these ads at auction, on which the calculated revenues depend). They are not the only indicators of user activity: the up/down "thumbs" under videos are also part of it, although they are not decisive in the ranking of videos. Along with comments, views are part of the diverse repertoire of signs in the media culture of evaluation.[4] Nevertheless, view counts are one of the main ways of reducing the multiplicity of cultural and documentary mediations to the realm of exchange value. They undergo a series of transmutations: they become an indicator of the popularity of a particular video in a Watch Page, a measure of subscriber demographics in YouTube Insights (now YouTube Analytics[5]), a marker of "popularity in the making" in YouTube Trends, or a unit of exchange—in the form of a ratio of views to money invested—for advertising formats in Google AdWords.

All of these devices give readability to views, which then become numerical values that rise more or less quickly, like one-way stock prices. They are linked to a limited set of information: for example, in the YouTube Trends screen, aggregation and comparison with other activities such as video-sharing, time-markers, and country breakdowns turn the numbers into "indicators" that allow us to monitor trends and derive strategies from them. The view turns out to be a powerful equivalence operator, making it possible to bring together a large number of entities in the same unit.[6] This process does not take place on the scale of a single medium considered as a support, but on the scale of groups of videos indexed on "themes," which in turn correspond to keywords. Unlike a newspaper or a TV channel, AdWords does not offer to associate the advertising format to a specific program or time slot, but to a "batch" of videos linked to keywords and to projected usage situations.

In addition to tying ad dollars to keywords or topics, advertisers can choose from a variety of ad formats: Specifically, InDisplay (for thumbnail displays among the required videos next to a viewed video), InSearch (for videos highlighted in search results), and InStream (a way to label pre-roll videos).[7] Finally, advertisers may prefer to use keywords, either by choosing them or selecting them from suggestions, to target specific searches or relatively specific videos. They may also choose to use pre-formatted themes that reflect the "interests" of users. This list of topics, which can be similar to a portal's list of topics, acts as a dictionary of the cultural and social worlds targeted by advertisers and defines the point where lifestyles meet their rephrasing in marketing speech (with categories such as "nightlife enthusiasts," "rock music enthusiasts").

Keywords, and even more so topics, serve as documentary markers for a multitude of pages and videos. A YouTube patent for a "video recommendation system" gives an idea of the logic behind the constitution of these aggregates.[8] The gestures of the Internet user (typing, interpreting, watching, listening, reading, clicking) are transformed into manipulable signals (inputs), into traces in visual databases of various kinds, and into operations in computer code. The targeting of Internet users and the assignment of advertisements to their "profiles" are based on this system: it shows how our online activities become *value labels* that allow the matching of advertisements with videos and the generation of revenue.

The phenomena tracked to contribute to the recommendations are very diverse: "user profile content," "user activity log content," and "video content history." They are further subdivided into "friendships," "group membership," "posted comments," "posted weblogs," "email," and "demographic information." The logics described by these graphs, as well as the various entity and algorithm models, are obviously constantly evolving in both logic and content. In fact, a white paper from YouTube's engineering team entitled "Deep Neural Network for YouTube Recommandations" (2016) states that way more categories are now taken into account, for "candidate generation" (the selection of relevant videos to display) as well as "ranking" (their ordering as "next video" and recommended videos in the right bar). Nevertheless, the patent gives a general idea: it is about crossing the activities of an Internet user with those of other users who have watched at least part of the same videos, as well as "user groups." In the process, at least some of the labels that are supposed to produce "personal" recommendations actually appear as predictable categories: "video genres" such as "comedy" or "music."

Thus, a series of mediations makes it possible to transform socially and semiotically "thick" signs and objects into relays in a circuit of transactions. Different realities or apparent realities, such as gestures, signs, videos, encrypted data, and keywords, are linked and processed according to principles of equivalence, and an important part of these processes is taken over by the "recommendation system." The calculability of things thus passes through a series of stages that give them their social and seemingly objective thickness. It is in this process that the market value of practices and videos is constituted, reinvented and distributed.

A Contested Standard

In patents, which in their own way represent the relations between all these situations, the view is worthwhile only because it makes it possible to give density to keywords and to rank them. However, this narrow perspective runs the risk of obscuring what is really essential, which is that the social significance of the "view" lies in the way it organizes broader processes and serves as a yardstick in references to popularity and creativity. The numbering of views functions as a mediating object. It turns the view into a sign of the accelerated circulation of music hits, materializes the goal of the musicians that YouTube claims to help, and testifies to the power of YouTube in the world of music (see Chapter 5).

In all these situations, the view and its numbers must be credible. Confidence in their ability to index something is the condition for these view counts to be effective: an audience measurement is not just an "artifact (let alone a manipulation) where the only thing that matters is the agreement between the parties; in order to be used, the measurement requires some form of plausibility."[9] This is the condition for the existence of a market, i.e. for the transformation of interpersonal relations of trust into systematic relations organized as transactions based on the principle of future benefit. The views counted by YouTube allow advertisers to bet that a video or a keyword will bring their message closer to the future curiosity and availability of YouTube visitors, and it allows artists to hope that, by releasing their music on the platform, they will gain a capital of fame and visibility that they can convert into other capitals in other situations.

Therefore, the view takes on a fiduciary value, which means that it constitutes a convention with its share of belief, an operator of equivalence, and at the same time a standard that gives its own weight to the whole system. What are these expectations based on? All the investments—symbolic and financial—in the view exist only because the following idea is recognized: at some point, the device has recorded something that has been translated into the incrementing of a counter of views, and then of other values in databases. If the view persists as a form of currency, it is because it is supposed to index something—but what exactly?

According to YouTube's text Impact Metrics published on the Creators Academy (2016),[10] a view was then primarily recorded and counted as a click somewhere on the playbar. Thus, it did not correspond to the continuous and qualified duration of a viewing or even a consumption. It was supposed to record a limited contact on a machine, transmit it via multiple protocols, and reconstruct it to be interpreted as the actualization of a punctual glance. Each click on the playback bar of a video, without reloading the page, was therefore counted as a "view": a consultation of a simple fragment of the video was consequently counted as a view. If the user clicked and then left, the gesture would still boost the view numbers.

"View" was thus the hyperbolic name given to this minimal point of contact, which guaranteed all the logical networks of processing and inference between "values" and all the transmutations between words, numbers and graphic symbols. The "view" could then be the object of trials that did not necessarily have the scope of a complete questioning of its essence. These trials were all the more important as the calculation of audience measurements became less and less a matter managed by experienced advertisers. Online media devices destabilized the figure of the consumer as a "quantified spectator, that convenient fiction on which everyone could agree," in favor of that of an Internet user who was sometimes difficult for professionals to characterize both in terms of his or her profile and activities.[11]

As a result, views became the target of public criticism, particularly in the music world, where their consistency and the conclusions they allowed were questioned. Ironically, this criticism was sometimes based on other indicators offered by YouTube: for example, the 64 million "views" counted in March 2011 for Rebecca Black's song "Friday" did not prevent more than 1 million dislikes (associated with the iconic thumbs-down button), leading music critics to break the link between "views" and popularity and to consecrate the video as "the most hated YouTube video of all time."[12] This episode draws attention to a video's ability to provoke a multiplicity of positions in order to inflate viewership numbers by perpetuating the confusion between audience measurement, public interest, and "taste" or satisfaction. In the production of reality shows, for example, "reaching the largest possible audience" is blatantly distinct from the idea of "pleasing the audience."[13] If there is no indication that Rebecca Black's song was released deliberately in anticipation of negative or polarized reactions, it marked an episode of awareness of this possible disjunction between "ratings" and "popularity" in the sense of a public response. Conversely, and illogically, this relationship, indifferent to any specific affect implied by the views, was nevertheless the one that YouTube chose to re-translate in a more positive framework, with the use of the word "interest" in AdSense screens for buying advertising space and in its technical patents.

Other, stronger criticisms of the status of "views" concerned the claim that they were a way of recording Internet users' activities. The press revealed that a star performer like Lady Gaga had managed to artificially inflate her view counts,[14] presumably with the help of third-party companies specializing in techniques such as lures, incentives associated with contests, and micro-payments to individuals participating in pyramid schemes or click farms.[15] This information has led YouTube to develop tools to detect these manipulative practices. While YouTube could not prevent them completely, the company acknowledged their existence to discourage them by criticizing their advertising effectiveness. It also ended up excluding paid video ads from its music charts (as surprising as it may seem, every advertised display of a music video was until then counted another view of the song in question).[16]

The company had issued several press releases on these issues, using the vocabulary of "quality control" and financial auditing to reassure advertisers. But YouTube was and remains structurally positioned as judge and jury, acting as both media company and advertising agency, research institute and even technical provider for the audits.[17] External agencies that would like to claim this control[18] are reduced to taking the data that YouTube provides through its API[19] and interpreting it in their own way, for example by crossing it with data from other websites. YouTube's insistence on reliability and certification could also be found in the promises of efficiency of advertising investments written on the pages dedicated to this purpose (YouTube For Advertisers), or through the aforementioned ratio of money to views in AdWords.

These promises were also based on a format and ad investment system that was original and specific to YouTube. Since its inception, online advertising formats have had very short life cycles, due to saturation, declining click-through rates, and the ingenuity of designers. To solve this problem, and to guarantee advertisers that the user had consciously chosen to watch their videos, YouTube proposed a system called "True View," a name that seemed to acknowledge the problem with the system. Thus, among the various formats available in the Google AdWords (now Google Ads) auctions, InStream was introduced. Initially offered for pre-roll videos, it is now available in mid-roll and post-roll options and called "True View In-Stream Ads." With this ad format, the advertiser pays only if the viewer is still watching an ad five seconds after launch, stays with it for at least thirty seconds or to the end of the video (whichever is shorter), or clicks on "cards" or other elements of the message. In this way, YouTube has implemented a kind of "non-zapping" that grounds the symbolic value of the view more effectively.

The exposure to advertising, insofar as it leads to records and traces as data, is part of what Arjun Appadurai calls commodities "by metamorphosis," i.e., things that are put into a state of commodity, even if this is not their original use[20]—in this case, it is not even certain that we can speak of "things" at all. Here, this metamorphosis is achieved through the engineering of inscriptions and symbols, which presents multiple points of discontinuity and fragility: the mere existence of a referent to the sign (as in the manipulation of "views"), the quality of the relation of the sign to the referent (the possibility of linking the counting of a click or a time spent with the phenomenological texture of a presence or an experience), or the qualification of the referent itself (how to identify what the click or the scrolling of a video is worth). This is why the combination of viewing times and keywords serves as a guarantee of a human activity whose psychological description can alternatively insist on phoric (the positive value of the thumbs up), sensory ("seeing"), cognitive ("interest"[21]), or affective (the comments, the case of Rebecca Black) dimensions.

For the rest of the Internet's users, and in particular its audience of publishers or channel managers and video producers, YouTube has enriched YouTube

Analytics by adding to the number of views an indicator of viewing time (Watch Time), often reinterpreted in advertising language as "Retention." Last but not least, its explanations of how views are counted now explain a two-step method that consists of running analytics on a video once it passes 300 views. No one knows the exact criteria behind this verification approach, but two hypotheses are regularly raised by online marketers who perform reverse engineering tests: one or more reloads of the page from the same IP address could block the increment, meaning that the "view" would refer less to a the actions of viewers in general and more to those of distinct viewer accounts, at least above a certain threshold; and the "click" criterion would actually be replaced by a minimum viewing time criterion (identified as between five and thirty seconds, depending on the source). Although this may seem justified by the need to prevent attempts at counterfeiting, one can only be surprised at the gap between the importance of this audience measurement in strategies for building online visibility and in payment flows (since YouTube's agreements for payment of advertising revenue are partly based on the number of views per video) and the lack of information about the exact procedures on which it is based.

In any case, the shift of economic value from the unit of a click (a "view") to a more precise count of time ("watch time" and "true views"), as well as the formulation of the continuity between user activity, clicks, and "interest," does not change the fundamental logic. YouTube claims to offer the best possible approximation of what Internet users do, desire, and feel, going through all the thickness and ambiguity involved in the manipulation of symbols and their articulation with the fabric of users' experience.

Purifying Experience

The counting of views by YouTube presupposes the existence of some idea of "exposure" to "content," a formalization of perception and an abstraction of time. These idealist categories are necessary in order to reduce the diversity of experiences of Internet users, viewers, and listeners to a single number and to give this number an advertising and financial value. It should be noted that the model of time as a commodity cannot be reduced to the result of technical modernity, nor to the assumption of an "attention economy." In fact, such a rationalization of time is at the heart of the capitalist labor contract: according to Karl Marx, labor power is reindexed in labor time and, once transformed in this way, becomes a commodity.[22] Since time-as-commodity is at the basis of the mode of production and exchange that defines a capitalist economy, it underpins the value of every product in this economic regime. It is precisely for this reason that some human activities can be reconsidered as commodities: "what makes the commodity exchangeable is the unit of abstract social labor time, because by reducing to the unit, one makes the abstraction of use value and needs."[23] Industrial and wage labor thus makes time itself one of the foundations of exchange value. From industrial labor to advertising, measured time can serve not only as a social convention, but also as an omnipresent economic value that translates other values.[24]

The re-characterization of the basis of "view" from simple "clicks" to "true views" and other verified "views" (through the presumption of an invested duration) has come to reveal precisely the fundamental symbolic and economic value implicit in the reference to "view." These variants construct the image of the "chosen time" of an invested, available, engaged Internet user, isolated from his or her environment, situated in an unaltered face-to-face with the video or piece of music being played, master of his or her consciousness to the point of actually making his or her intensive actions coincide with those of a homogeneous calculation of time. In this paradigm, not only is the duration specific to the experience of a work itself regulated by the measurable time of a recording, but the different potential experiences of a work by different individuals become commensurable between them. This fiction of objective, equal and dedicated listening or consumption is at odds with the variety of practices Internet users: they are not necessarily present or attentive when a piece of music is "playing", and thus experience musical or advertising in a more non-linear/ discontinuous/fluid way than what a category like "Watch Time" suggests. But this representation of time-as-commodity does not account for the actual experiences of more dedicated listeners/spectators either. When one has a "crush" on a particular song (or a "shock," as Walter Benjamin qualified the experience of the movies[25]), or when one appreciates music by thinking/feeling through the articulation of the totality of a musical works and its parts (referred to by Adorno as "structural listening"), one experiences how music shifts the qualitative experience of duration itself, thus rendering musical experience irreducible to "exposure for x amount of time to content y."[26]

Counting clicks as views in order to display them on pages, certifying true views to advertisers because they exceed a zapping time (true view), or counting watch time in order to deduct views for channel editors and rights-holders: all of these operations not only try to account for what Internet users do when they launch videos, but also promise from the outset a "purified" attention, isolated from any interference, tuned to a chosen object. To associate music with this ideal, then, is simply to extend this quantitative model of perception by adding the lack of distinction between sensory faculties or techniques: if the activity of looking is reduced theoretically to a measurable and enumerable activity—to pure *viewing*—then the sensory technique of hearing/listening may well be nothing but a view.

For Jonathan Crary, Fechner's formalization of vision expresses "the proximity, or even coincidence, of sensory experience and an economic and social terrain dominated by exchange values,"[27] in which the devices for measuring vision "make it possible to control the perceiving subject, to predict it, to make it productive, and above all to bring it into line with the other domains of rationalization."[28] Hearing has undergone a similar kind of scientific "purification." Even before the psycho-physical model, the idea of an auditory perception adequate to the work and valued as such was already inscribed in the Western tradition of discourses on music, whether in the dominance of the discourse on music as a rhetoric of affects in the eighteenth century, in the gradual valorization of a clear and distinct attention in which reason guides the senses in the nineteenth century,[29] or in the discourse on aesthetic listening in the twentieth century.

The way in which scientists and engineers imagined hearing as a trans-individual phenomenon that could be objectified and measured by numbers thus resonated with the ideal of rationality of specifically musical and "classical" hearing. The invention of sound as a transversal dimension of music and language, as opposed to noise, responds to the exclusion of "any precise content" in vision, which had already allowed a "homogenization" with the other senses.[30] Indeed, it is because of such a purification that Georg Simmel, at the beginning of the twentieth century, was able to assume that an aesthetic taste could be explained by a quantitative factor of physiological "excitement."[31]

YouTube's work on audience measurement is part of this dynamic. On the one hand, these remarks shed light on the definitions and implicit hierarchies of sensory capacities that feed economic practices. Because vision has proven historically to be objectifiable and manageable, especially through video players and audience measurement, the instruments of its management and control can be renewed and adapted from one media device to another. On the other hand, the success of the enterprise of scientific quantification and imaginary homogenization of sensory faculties has caused them to lose some of their specificity in the social imaginary, and this is why today we can value relations to mediatized music as views or time spent on the basis of a similar projection: an available and interested media consumer.

From the point of view of the display of advertising on YouTube, the difference between seeing and hearing does not matter: a piece of music in the media player starts like any other video, and it does not matter whether it is watched or enjoyed according to different sensory techniques. As mentioned above, the match between advertising and recordings is mainly semantic, through keywords, in a logic that motivates the ubiquitous word of "content." The categories of "affinity audiences" sold to advertisers (such as "rock enthusiasts") are situated at the level of consumption practices, of musical genres as realities that cross media and are well encapsulated in video formats as moving images (music videos, music lessons): they are never linked to dispositions that stem from a specific culture of recorded sound or music listening as such. In fact, this vagueness would be a problem only if YouTube wanted to sell its advertisers on receptive, present, actually *listening* users as such, rather than a more blurry idea of the "time spent" by aggregated audience profiles gathered around specified "interests."

Traffic As Value

If the view is nothing more than a unit of consumption that derives watch time from "indifferent" machine time, how can we know whether this time should be interpreted virtually as a time (watch time) for listening/consuming music or primarily for video? And why does this difference matter? The difference is important for two reasons. The first is that, contrary to the thesis of a structural indifference of "platforms" to cultural practices, and as we have seen in the previous chapters, YouTube has built part of its strategy on demonstrating its capacity to act as a cultural force for musicians, to promote professional practices of musicianship (YouTube for Artists) as well as music listening and discovery (YouTube Music). If the company is not able to distinguish a relationship to music as a listening experience at its infrastructural levels, then it undermines its discourse as a tool for music discovery and/or music distribution, and this may limit its credibility and claim to mediate music culture rather than just distributing music videos. After all, not every record label or musician is equipped or wants to compete in a space organized to promote music videos first and foremost. But more importantly, music's presence on YouTube still depends on the agreement of record companies and other rights-holders for the platform to exploit their catalogs. And that agreement in turn depends on YouTube's ability to convince its music partners that it is capable of valuing music as such, not just music video "content."

In 2014, YouTube addressed the specificity of music when counting views. Tracks submitted through the channel of an "official artist" or a partner such as a music distributor are subject to a special statistical calculation (An "Official Artist" account for a musician or performer goes through a different process that requires first having the "Topic Channel" generated in their name by YouTube based on criteria such as number of videos, number of views, and the "quality" associated with an artist name. It is then necessary to create a channel in the name of the artist, performer, or musician and to apply for qualification by e-mail to YouTube. As of the writing of this book, to become eligible for the "Partner program," which authorizes "monetization" through advertising, the channel must have achieved 4,000 hours of viewing over the previous twelve months and a minimum of 1,000 subscribers.) The total number of views for a given track includes the number of views of videos that use all or part of the track, including official videos, live videos, fan-generated content (and in the past, promotions or advertising[32]). Each view of a video that includes a song (declared by the rights-holders as a composition or recording[33]) is therefore counted as a view for that artist and that song, regardless of how long the song is in the video or how it is used: it is the "view" (again, not a mere click anymore but an unknown minimum playing time) of the video that includes the song that counts. These views are therefore not necessarily linked to a type of video, such as a recorded archive or an official music video, that anchors the music in the culture of listening or of musical media. According to this principle, a piece of music could go unnoticed and even be disliked in a video that is successful for other reasons, without this affecting its view count. It can also become successful simply by being used in a video satire, as a theme song, a funny jingle, or as any kind of background music.

Of course, it is difficult to weigh the relative importance of this metric against other factors that affect the rise of particular songs or pieces of music in recommendation systems, such as media exposure in other spaces, cumulative viewership on different video formats for the same song, or the influence of product placements (which do affect video rankings). What is important, however, is the way in which, under a seemingly consensual lexical reference like "view," a mode of calculation can alter the values that make some musical works famous and from which artists can derive income. The determination of the value of musical works through sales figures, radio, and local broadcasts—which themselves depend on contested and relatively evolving modes of calculation—is anchored above all in the idea of a taste linked to "consumption practices," even if they are indirect or reconstructed. On YouTube—although it is difficult in practice to distinguish between views and actual consumption practices—internal traffic, as a result of the music circulating on the platform, has become a potentially determining criterion. This is consistent with the recommendation system, which tends to favor, in addition to the inclusion of videos in "YouTube channels" with frequent publications, phenomena such as the initial speed of spreading, the intersection between several different topics and domains,[34] or polarizing themes.[35]

Of course, this mechanism works as an incentive for rights-holders to authorize the reappropriation of their pieces in order to benefit from the exposure of these charts, or even to ensure that they are promoted with the help of companies that follow the steps of Dance On, initiating pseudo-spontaneous dance videos as part of the promotion of singles, hoping for a snowball effect. According to this logic, it doesn't matter what space is reserved for sound and music as a form in the experience by someone approaching the video: what counts is the music's ability to trigger covers, remixes, or appearances in a new video, for example because it can be easily edited with images or because it has a strong evocative power.

As a tendency, any piece of music that is covered or serves as background in many successful videos is likely to compete with a piece of music that does not allow for this kind of derivative use. This can be seen as a *meme-ing* of music, which consists in betting on the articulation between a piece of music and the contagion of an image, even a parodic one, to accelerate its circulation. Such a logic now dominates the functioning of the successful application TikTok, which also made the most of YouTube's early focus on amateurish choreography, the playful use of audio/video sync, as well as tools that push song covers by design the design of embedding a previous video in a new one being a distant echo of YouTube's forgotten "video response" function (linking two productions to each other, one as "source" and the other as a "response").[36]

As we can see, views are a fragile edifice that supports audience measurement and defines the value of music. Counting the success of music videos as views is not an indication of the primacy of the visual over the aural, nor of a total indifference to YouTube's "content"—on the contrary, I have shown how the semantics attached to video are constantly used and translated to constitute audiences. "View" as a word rather points out in a straightforward way that on YouTube, music takes on its social and economic value without having to be grasped separately from its visual and thematic associations—even without being appreciated or even simply heard as such. But the word only goes so far and does not convey that, in YouTube's logic, what matters most is how music generates its own traffic: music is ranked and valued on the basis of the attractiveness of the videos in which it participates.

The fate of music on YouTube depends not only on its social potential, but also on its ability to merge with other forms of expression and to seek relationships with videos that do not necessarily see sound and music as specific phenomena—to serve purposes other than its own. In this respect, the frequent criticisms of a "value gap" (between what YouTube supposedly earns from the presence of music and what the rights-holders collect) have limited relevance. They focus on the gap between the (use/experiential) value of music as a commodity and the revenue stream that the company allows for it (the thousandths of a cent that YouTube pays out from advertising purchases, keeping more than half, officially, to cover its own expenses). But what should be at stake, more than this disparity, is the very method of measuring views, and the ways in which revenue distribution and the valuation of music are made dependent on it. Indeed, a more fundamental question is whether the value of music should really depend on its ability to circulate at high intensity and raise the stakes in advertising auctions. Since the completion of this book, the rise of YouTube Music as a subscription service has been an obvious compensation, if not a definitive answer, to this complex relationship of YouTube (as a broader video platform) with music culture and commerce.

Conclusion

Some will argue that there is nothing new under the sun, and they may be right. YouTube was not the first technology company to demonstrate an opportunistic relationship with culture and music to further its own ends. A few years ago, Maria Eriksson and her colleagues showed how the Swedish company Spotify was built from the ground up on a model of data collection and ad sales, with music as bait and an afterthought for its founders.[1] More broadly, in conditions where the tendency of tech companies to pivot at the slightest opportunity meets the massive diffusion of online listening practices, their attempts to mobilize music in one way or another-whether as simple "content" to host, as a subject to communicate about, or to inspire the development of specific tools and infrastructure-have proven less and less surprising.[2] Of course, this book can only scratch the surface of the ways in which music has played a role in the development and rise of YouTube. I wanted to focus on the platform's most structural dimensions, emphasizing how music helped define the kind of audience and experience it was built for, how it defined its strategic positioning as a patron of artists and creators, and how it extended its reach through the nexus of copyright control and audience measurement.

Even though I began by reversing the usual, deterministic account of YouTube "shaping" music culture, the attentive reader would have noticed that I did not go so far as to minimize how the process also worked to define a specific objecthood and values for music on YouTube. Rather than a pure reversal, each chapter also proposed a way of thinking about how YouTube has framed the experience of music. However, I was careful to always explain these stories as an ongoing process of evolution, and not as definitive, one-way transformations, and to connect them to broader stories about relationships to music and trends in the music industry and music culture. The main objective was to propose a critique of the discourse of digital media transformations, in the sense of the classic "critique of political economy"—to weaken the theoretical foundations of such a discourse—but also in the sense of discerning nuances within the same object: not underestimating the changes, but also not neglecting what precedes them, contradicts them, and goes beyond them. Indeed, even when YouTube was the most "disruptive" in its claims, it often mobilized, captured, capitalized on, and reoriented multiple practices and knowledge around music culture and commerce whose grounds had been defined elsewhere. In the end, when YouTube embeds music in a project built around the potential of video technologies, when it reconfigures rationalization and competitive market logics, it is not so much transcending the music industry as repeating some of its classic moves. As a company, we can even say that it is repeating its inaugural period. In fact, YouTube takes us back to the origins of the music industry, far beyond the confines of the major record companies: the early inventors of devices like Edison or Berliner, as well as the early electrical and radio network companies like RCA, had indeed chosen to invest in culture and media, to create record labels and musical programming, to develop a vast market of song covers in order to turn their inventions into commercial outlets and hope to sell them to a large audience. YouTube has finally repeated the approach of these pioneers in the cross-industrialization of culture, technology and media: like its competitors in music streaming, the company relies on a double movement of intensifying the circulation of culture and strengthening the control of its supports. At a time when this movement of control is being reinforced decisively, it is worth noting that much of the most valuable music of the twentieth century—both avant-garde and pop— was built on a certain reflexivity towards these processes. An expanded critique of music's role in shaping technological and media platforms will mean paying attention to the ways in which music enacts this critique from within, and the ways in which some of its currents advance particular relationships to listening, sharing, and sociality.

Notes

Where the author has been unable to verify the URL visited in the entries below, the word [online] appears.

Introduction

1   Sarah Lacy. *The Stories of Facebook, YouTube and MySpace: The People, the Hype and the Deals Behind the Giants of Web 2.0.* (s.l.): Crimson Publishing, 2009.

1   From Music Boxes to the YouTube Player (2000–05)

1   Steve Collins and Sherman Young. *Beyond 2.0: the Future of Music.* (Bristol, CT: Equinox Publishing, 2014.)

2   Jeremy Wade Morris. *Selling Digital Music, Formatting Culture* (Oakland, California: University of California Press, 2015.)

3   Raymond Williams and Ederyn Williams. *Television: Technology and Cultural Form.* (London and New York: Routledge, 2003.)

4   Jeremy Wade Morris. *Selling Digital Music* (Berkeley, CA: University of California Press. 2015.)

5   Jeremy Wade Morris and Evan Elkins. "There's a History for That: Apps and Mundane Software as Commodity," *The Fibreculture Journal* 25 (2015): 63–88.

6   Jacqueline Emigh. "New Flash Player Rises in the Web-Video Market", *Computer* vol. 39, no. 2 (2006): 14–16.

7   Tim O'Reilly. "What Is Web 2.0. Design Patterns and Business Models for the Next Generation of Software." *OReilly.com*, September 30, 2015, https://www.oreilly.com/pub/a/web2/archive/what-is-web-20.html.

8   Tyler Woods. "How The Hype Machine Has Persisted And Endured." *Technical.ly* [online]. July 2, 2017.

9   Victor Keegan. "Will MySpace ever lose its monopoly?" *The Guardian* [online]. August 2, 2007.

10 Andrew Goldstone, "MP3 Blogs: A Silver Bullet for the Music Industry or a Smoking Gun for Copyright Infringement," *SSRN Electronic Journal,* 2006; David Seilder. "The Right to Copyright?: Mp3 Blogs and the Rise of the Online Taste-Maker," *SSRN Electronic Journal,* 2010; Patrick O'Donnell and Steven McClung. "MP3 Music Blogs: Their Efficacy in Selling Music and Marketing Bands," *Atlantic Journal of Communication* vol.16, no. 2 (2008): 71–87.

11 Jawed Karim. *r   p 2006: YouTube: From Concept To Hypergrowth* [online]. January 10, 2006.

12 Jean-Samuel Beuscart. "Sociabilité en ligne, notoriété virtuelle et carrière artistique: Les usages de MySpace par les musiciens autoproduits." *Réseaux,* vol. 152, no. 6 (2008): 139.

13 Dan Perkel. "Copy and Paste Literacy? Literacy Practices in the Production of a MySpace Profile," in *Informal learning and digital media,* ed. Kirsten Drotner, Hans Siggaard Jensen and Kim Schrøder. (Newcastle, UK: Cambridge Scholars, 2008), 21–3.

14 GIGA OM. *Chad Hurley: How We Did It* [online]. 2013.

15 Carlo Longino. "So that's why MySpace blocked YouTube." *Techdirt* [online], October 1, 2006.

16 "MySpace Re-Enables YouTube Embeds." *YouTube Blog* [online]. December 23, 2006.

17 INTERNCRAIG. *How to Upload a Video* [online]. September 6, 2005.

18 Irina Shklovski and D. Boyd. "Music as Cultural Glue: Supporting Bands and Fans on MySpace." *Unpublished Tech Report.* 2006.

19 Jeremy D. Larson. "Lyrics as your aim away message: an appreciation," *Pitchfork,* June 10, 2007.

20 Last.fm   Play music, find songs, and discover artists [online].

21 Arjun Appadurai. "Introduction: commodities and the politics of value," *The Social Life of Things.* (Cambridge: Cambridge University Press, 1986), 11–18.

22 Étienne Candel, Valérie Jeanne-Perrier, and Emmanuël Souchier. "Petites formes, grands desseins: d'une grammaire des énoncés éditoriaux à la standardisation des écritures," in Jean Davallon (ed.), *L'économie des écritures sur le Web.* (Cachan: Hermès Science publications-Lavoisier, 2012), 165–201. See also Samuel Goyet. *De briques et de blocs. La fonction éditoriale des interfaces de program- mation (API) web: entre science combinatoire et industrie du texte.* PhD thesis. Paris: Celsa Paris-Sorbonne, November 22, 2017, p. 54.

2 Music, Incidentally (2005–09)

1 Michel Chion. *L'audio-vision: son et image au cinéma*. (Paris: Armand Colin, 2014), 101.

2 Joost Broeren. "Digital Attractions: Reloading Early Cinema in Online Video Collections," in Patrick Vondereau and Pelle Snickars (eds), *The YouTube Reader* (Stockholm: National Library of Sweden, 2009), 154.

3 Rainer Hillrichs. *Poetics of Early YouTube: Production, Performance, Success* [online]. PhD thesis, Faculty of Philosophy. Universitäts- und Landesbibliothek Bonn: Universitäts- und Landesbibliothek Bonn, 2005, p. 98.

4 https://www.digitalmusicnews.com/2015/09/09/how-signing-a-major-record-deal-nearly-destroyed-my-music-career/

5 Karim Jawed. *Me at the zoo – YouTube* [online], April 23, 2005.

6 Hillrichs, *Poetics of Early YouTube*.

7 François J. Bonnet. *Les mots et les sons: un archipel sonore* (Paris: Éditions de l'éclat, 2012), 218.

8 SEBIII. *Music drives it crazy . . .* [online]. August 25, 2005.

9 David Firth. *The Incredible Mouth Band* [online]. September 17, 2006.

10 Cf. Sophie Maisonneuve. *L'invention du disque: 1877–1949; genèse de l'usage des médias musicaux contemporains*. (Paris: Éd. des Archives Contemporaines, 2009). Lydia Goehr. *Le musée imaginaire des œuvres musicales* (Paris: La Rue Musicale, 2018). Roger Chartier. *L'ordre des livres: lecteurs, auteurs, bibliothèques en Europe entre XIVe et XVIIIe siècle* (Aix-en-Provence: Alinea, 1992).

11 Introducing YouTube Director. *YouTube Blog* [online]. April 10, 2006.

12 Tarleton Gillespie. "Governance Of and By platforms," in *The Sage Handbook of Social Media*, ed. Jean Burgess, Alice Marwick, Thomas Poell (Thousand Oaks, CA: SAGE, 2017).

13 Jean-Samuel Beuscart. "Sociabilité online, notoriété virtuelle et carrière artistique: Les usages de MySpace par les musiciens autoproduits," *Réseaux*, vol. 152, no. 6 (2008): 139.

14 Hunter Walk. "The Time When Lady Gaga Told YouTube to Keep Its UX 'Shitty' (& Some Snapchat Thoughts)." *Hunter Walk blog* [online]. May 28, 2015.

15 Hillrichs, *Poetics of Early YouTube*.

16 Mark Greif. *Against Everything: Essays*. (New York: Pantheon Books, 2016), 501–02.

17 Michaël Bourgatte. "Le mashup et la transtextualité audiovisuelle sur Internet," *Communication & langages* no. 4 (2019): 97–114.

18 KONEFKU. *Man dancing* [online]. August 4, 2005.

19 Jawed Karim. *Jawed Karim, Illinois Commencement, pt.2* [online]. May 6, 2007.
20 Steven Feld. "A Sweet Lullaby for World Music." *Public Culture* [online], vol. 12, no. 1 (2000): 145–71.
21 IMDB. *Deep Forest: Sweet Lullaby* [online]. 1993.
22 Shirley Ellis, "The Clapping Song (Clap Pat Clap Slap)." *Discogs* [online]. [n.d.].
23 Nathan McAlone. "Madonna cofounded a startup that manufactures viral dance trends – and 'Whip/Nae Nae' was its first monster hit." *Business Insider France* [online]. January 1, 2016.
24 Kieran Press-Reynolds. "How TikTok Is Taking the Tunes out of Pop". *Highsnobiety* [online]. March 12, 2020.
25 Peter Szendy. *Tubes: la philosophie dans le juke-box* (Paris: Éditions de Minuit, 2008).

3 Competing for Fun (2006–13)

1 *Variété* [online]. ATILF CNRS & Université de Lorraine, 2017.
2 Derek B. Scott *Sounds of the Metropolis* (New York: Oxford University Press, 2008), 54.
3 EEPYBIRD. *Extreme Mentos & Diet Coke* [online]. May 1, 2006.
4 ERB. *James Bond vs Austin Powers – Epic Rap Battles of History* [online]. June 14, 2016.
5 Henry Jenkins. "YouTube & The Vaudeville Aesthetic." *henryjenkins.org* [online]. November 19, 2006.
6 ENTERTAINEMENT, Thrillist. "The 100 Greatest YouTube Videos of All Time, Ranked." *Thrillist* [online]. June 14, 2018.
7 *Vaudeville* [online]. ATILF CNRS & Université de Lorraine, 2017.
8 Jason Laipply. *Evolution of Dance* [online]. April 6, 2006.
9 Jason Laipply. *Judson Laipply, Live on* Oprah [online]. March 17, 2015.
10 "Code of Best Practices in Fair Use for Online Video." *Center for Media and Social Impact* [online]. [n.d.].
11 Jean Burgess, Joshua Green, and Henry Jenkins. *YouTube: Online Video and Participatory Culture* (Oxford: Wiley, 2013), 91.
12 Saul Hansell. "Technology: Joining the Party, Eager to Make Friends." *The New York Times*, October 16, 2006.
13 Lara Langer Cohen, *Going Underground. Race, Space, and the Subterranean in the Nineteenth-Century United States* (Durham, NC: Duke University Press, 2023).

14 Cf. Dick Hebdige. *Sous-culture: le sens du style* (Paris: La Découverte, 2008). Sarah Thornton. *Club Cultures: Music, Media, and Subcultural Capital* (Hanover, NH: University Press of New England, 1996).

15 YouTube—Broadcast Yourself. *YouTube.com* [online]. September 28, 2006.

16 *YouTube "Underground" Contest Rules, Terms & Conditions* [online]. December 2, 2006.

17 Thorton, *Club Cultures.*

18 Emily I. Dolan. "'. . . This little ukulele tells the truth': Indie pop and kitsch authenticity." *Popular Music* [online], vol. 29, no. 3 (2010): 457–69.

19 ,David Hesmondhalgh. "Post-Punk's attempt to democratise the music industry: the success and failure of Rough Trade." *Popular Music* [online], vol. 16, no. 3 (1997): 255.

20 Gérôme Guibert. *Indie-pop. Analyse d'un courant musical.* 1996.

21 "Out From the Underground." *YouTube Blog* [online]. December 13, 2006.

22 Virginia Heffernan. "YouTube Awards the Top of Its Heap." *New York Times.* March 27, 2007.

23 Ramya Raghavan. "Make voting go viral." *YouTube Blog* [online]. September 2, 2012.

24 Matt Stahl. "A moment like this: American Idol and narratives of meritocracy," in Christopher J. Washburne and Maiken Derno (eds), *Bad Music: The Music We Love to Kate* (New York: Routledge, 2013).

25 "When you enter the community page on YouTube, one of the first words you see is 'contest'." Jens Schöter. "On the logic of the digital archive," in Patrick Vonderau and Pelle Snickars (eds), *The YouTube Reader* (Stockholm: National Library of Sweden, 2009) 154–66.

26 Mathew Ingram. "Who is Tay Zonday?". *The Globe and Mail.* August 15, 2007.

27 David Grossman. "YouTube Live: a disastrous spectacle Google would like you to forget." *The Verge* [online]. November 1, 2013.

28 Ibid.

29 Ibid.

30 THE YOUTUBE TEAM. "The Ups and Downs of Music Licensing for YouTube." *You- Tube Help* [online]. December 19, 2008. Chris Maxy. "Warner Music Comes Back to YouTube." *YouTube Blog* [online]. September 29, 2009.

31 Keynote Address at the MIPCOM conference, the world's audiovisual content market. *YouTube Blog* [online]. October 25, 2008.

32 Weezer. *Weezer—Pork And Beans* [online]. November 13, 2009.

33 Ramya Raghavan. "Election results and trends, live on YouTube tonight." *Official YouTube Blog* [online]. February 11, 2010.

34 Robert Kyncl. "More great content creators coming to YouTube." *Official YouTube Blog* [online]. October 29, 2011.

35 NAKASHIMA, Ryan. "YouTube launching 100 new channels." *USATODAY.COM* [online]. October 29, 2011.

36 Todd Spangler. "YouTube Music Awards Nominees Announced." *Variety* [online]. January 2013.

37 Maria San Filippo. "A Cinema Of Recession: Micro-budgeting, microdrama, and the 'mumblecore' movement." *Cineaction* [online], no. 85 (2011): 2–8.

38 Patrice Blouin. "Sur l'art du clip de Spike Jonze." *Cahiers du Cinema* vol. 14, no. 651 (2009): 33.

4 From Choosing to Streaming (2008–14)

1 David Chaney. "Le grand magasin comme forme culturelle." *Réseaux* [online], vol. 14, no. 80 (1996): 81–96.

2 Robin James. "Songs of myself." *Audimat* no. 12 (2019): 105-123.

3 Ben Popper. "YouTube Music is here, and it's a game changer." *The Verge* [online]. December 11, 2015.

4 H. Stith Bennett and Howard Saul Becker. *On Becoming a Rock Musician* (New York: Columbia University Press, 2017).

5 THE YOUTUBE MUSIC TEAM. "Music on YouTube that hits the right note." *YouTube Blog* [online]. December 11, 2014.

6 A.J. Frank. "YouTube Just Got Hotter: Views Added to Billboard's Charts." *YouTube Blog* [online]. February 21, 2013.

7 Elliot Von Buskirk. "The Man Who Invented Scrobbling and Changed the World." *WIRED* [online]. November 20, 2012.

8 Kevin Alloca. "Introducing YouTube Trends." *YouTube Blog* [online]. December 20, 2010.

9 Tarleton Gillespie. "#trendingistrending: when algorithm become culture," in Robert Seyfert and Jonathan Roberts (eds), *Algorithmic Cultures: Essays on Meaning, Performance and New Technologies*, 1st edn (London and New York: Routledge, 2016), 54.

10 Hunter Walk. "'Your Site Has a Cadence': The Best Blog Post from 2012 You Never Read." *Hunter Walk blog* [online]. February 10, 2014.

11 Popper, "YouTube Music is here."

12 *Spotify for Brands* [online]. [n.d.].

13 Sam Gutelle. "YouTube, With Bigger Plans, Gets Set To Shut Down Its Music Disco." *Tubefilter.com* [online]. October 24, 2014.

5 The Streamlining of Expression (2014–18)

1 Jin Kin. "The institutionalization of YouTube: From user-generated content to profes- sionally generated content." *Media, Culture & Society* vol. 34, no. 1 (2012): 53–67.

2 Heather McIntosh. "Vevo and the Business of Online Music Video Distribution." *Popular Music and Society* vol. 39, no. 5 (2016): 487–500.

3 John Seabrook. "Streaming Dreams. YouTube turns pro." *New-Yorker* [online]. January 16, 2012.

4 Jason Toynbee. *Making Popular Music* (London: Bloomsbury, 2000).

5 Seabrook, "Streaming Dreams."

6 Vincent Bullich. "Régulation des pratiques amateurs et accompagnement de la professionnalisation: la stratégie de YouTube dans la course aux contenus exclusifs." *Les Enjeux de l'Information et de la Communication* no. 16 (2015): 27–42.

7 Philippe Bouquillion, Bernard Miège, and Pierre Moeglin. "Industries du contenu et industries de la communication. Contribution à une déconstruction de la notion de créativité." *Les Enjeux de l'Information et de la Communication* [online], no. 16 (2018): 17–26.

8 Keynote Address at the MIPCOM conference, the world's audiovisual content market. *YouTube Blog* [online]. October 25, 2008.

9 Stuart Dredge. "Live from Music 4.5: YouTube talks music videos (#m4pt5)." *Musically.com* [online]. November 26, 2013.

10 Alex Carloss. "Investing in creativity." *Official YouTube Blog* [online]. September 18, 2014.

11 Augustin Girard. "Les industries culturelles: un handicap ou une nouvelle chance pour le développement culturel?," in UNESCO, *Les industries culturelles: un enjeu pour l'avenir de la culture* (Paris: Unesco, 1982) 21–36.

12 Dan Schwabel. "Inside the Brand of Justin Bieber: An Interview with Manager Scooter Braun." *Forbes.com* [online]. February 11, 2011.

13 Mark Fisher. *K-Punk: The Collected and Unpublished Writings of Mark Fisher (2004–2016)* (XX: Repeater, 2018).

14 Edgar Morin, *L'esprit du temps* (Paris: Grasset, 1962). Jeremy Gilbert and Ewan Pearson. *Discographies: Dance Music, Culture and the Politics of Sound* (London: Psychology Press, 1999). Simon Frith. "The Industrialization of Popular Music," in Andy Bennet, Barry Shank, and Jason Toynbee (eds), *The Popular Music Studies Reader* (London: Routledge, 2006).

15 Thomas Grignon. "Quand Google fait école. Une prétention pédagogique en question," *Communication & Langages* [online], vol. 188, no. 2 (2016): 123–39.

16 Hillrichs, *Poetics of Early YouTube.*

17 Toynbee, *Making Popular Music.*

18 Lucas Shaw. "YouTube's Unlikely Peacemaker Has a Plan to Make Musicians Rich." *Bloomberg.com* [online]. January 3, 2018.

19 Angela McRobbie. *Be Creative: Making a Living in the New Culture Industries* (Hoboken, NJ: Wiley, 2018), 85.

20 Mark Fisher. *Ghosts of My Life: Writings on Depression, Hauntology and Lost Futures* (Alresford: John Hunt Publishing, 2014).

21 Jeremy Wade Morris. "Music Platforms and the Optimization of Culture," *Social Media + Society* vol. 6, no. 3 (2020).

22 In the United States, this term describes payments or confidential gifts given by record companies to programmers to ensure that their artists appear on playlists.

23 Antony Bruno. "YouTube stars don't always welcome record deals." *Reuters* [online]. February 26, 2007 [June 11, 2018].

24 Cours: Renforcez les liens qui vous unissent à vos fans. *YouTube Creators* [online].

25 "Build A Career." *YouTube for Artists* [online]. [n.d.].

26 Jessie Scoullar. "Which is the best direct-to-fan platform?" in *Music Industry Insights, Midem* [online]. October 8, 2014.

27 WATSON, Allan et WARD, Jenna. Op.cit.

28 Arlie Russell Hochschild, Salomé Fournet-Fayas, and Cécile Thomé. *Le prix des sentiments: au coeur du travail émotionnel* (Paris: La Découverte, 2017).

29 Hesmondhalgh, "Post-Punk."

30 "Involve your fans." *YouTube for Artists* [online; n.d.].

31 Karine Berthelot-Guiet. "Extension du domaine de la conversation: discours de marque et publicitarité," *Communication & Langages* [online] vol. 169, no. 3 (2011): 77–86.

32 Dallas W. Smythe. "On the audience commodity and its work," *Media and Cultural Studies: Keywords* (1981), 230–56.

6 The Hit Machine Narrative (2012–18)

1 Laurent Carpentier. "YouTube, machine à tubes." *LeMonde.fr* [online]. October 31, 2013.

2 Benjamin Chapon. "Madéon, le phénomène Youtube de 2012, sort son premier album." *20minutes.fr* [online]. March 31, 2015.

3   McAlone, "Madonna cofounded a startup."

4   Meaghan Garvey. "The Influencer: A Decade of Soulja Boy." *Pitchfork* [online]. July 9, 2015. Damien Scott. "Opinion: Why You Should Bow Down To Soulja Boy, Pioneer Of Hip- Hop's Digital Revolution." *Vibe.com* [online]. August 29, 2013.

5   https://blog.youtube/news-and-events/a-youtube-built-just-for-music/

6   Catherine Saouter. "Battle At Kruger," in Jean Davallon (ed.), *L'économie des écritures sur le Web* (Paris: Lavoisier, 2012), 37–50.

7   "How Musician Maggie Rogers Landed a Viral Hit on YouTube," [online], http://youtube-trends.blogspot.com.

8   Sianne Ngai. *Our Aesthetic Categories: Zany, Cute, Interesting* (Cambridge, MA: Harvard University Press, 2015).

9   https://journals.openedition.org/volume/docannexe/image/6141/img-1.png

10 https://journals.openedition.org/volume/docannexe/image/6141/img-2.png

11 Alex Siber. "Daily Discovery: Maggie Rogers Perfects a Dance-Folk Blend With Anticipated Single 'Alaska," *Pigeons & Planes* [online]. https://pigeonsandplanes. com/+discover/+2016/+06/ aggie-rogers-alaska/ aggie-rogers-alaska-2. June 15, 2016 (visited October 8, 2018).

12 Dexter Thomas. "Snack Trax: Finally, that song Pharrell was freaking out about has been released," *Los Angeles Times* [online]. http://www.latimes.com/+la-et-ms-snacktrax-maggie-rogers-father-20160615-snap-htmlstory.html. June 23, 2016 (visited October 8, 2018).

13 Marissa Martinelli. "Listen to Maggie Rogers' 'Alaska' (aka the Song That Blew Pharrell Away)," *Slate* [online]. http://www.slate.com/+blogs/+browbe at/+2016/+06/+16/+. June 16, 2016.

14 Daniel Barrow. "A Plague Of Soars. Warps In The Fabric Of Pop," *The Quietus* [online]. http://thequietus.com/+articles/+06073-a-plague-of-soars-warps-in-the-fabric-of-pop. April 13, 2001 (visited June 6, 2018).

15 Vulture Editors, " 7 Best New Songs of the Week." *Vulture.com*, June 21, 2016, online: http://www.vulture.com.

16 Audrey White. "Pharrell's Stunned Face Launched Maggie Rogers' Career. Now What ?," Pitchfork [online]. https://pitchfork.com/+thepitch/+1206-pharrells-stunned-face-launched-maggie-rogers-career-now-what/+. June 26, 2016 (visited June 11, 2018).

17 Doug Schardt. *LinkedIn.com* [online]. https://www.linkedin.com/in/doug-schardt-410811b6/.

18 "How Musician Maggie Rogers Landed a Viral Hit on YouTube," http://youtube-trends.blogspot.com.

7 (Semi-)Automating Authorship (2007–18)

1 Ibid., 68.

2 Patrick Burkart and Tom McCourt. "Infrastructure for the Celestial Jukebox," *Popular Music* vol. 23, no. 3 (2004): 349–62.

3 The YouTube Team. "The Ups and Downs of Music Licensing for YouTube." *YouTube Help* [online]. December 19, 2008.

4 "Manage your rights at scale." *Creator Academy* [online]. [n.d.].

5 Hunter Walk. "Copy, remix, profit: How YouTube & Shapeways Are Inventing the Future of Copyright". *Hunter Walk blog* [online]. September 25, 2014.

6 Ibid.

7 Ibid.

8 Alain Supiot. *La gouvernance par les nombres: cours au Collège de France*, 2012–2014 (Paris: Fayard, 2015)

9 Vincent Bullich. "Perspectives critiques sur la propriété artistique." *Les Enjeux de l'Information et de la Communication* no. 14/3A (2013): 81–97.

10 Pierre-Carl Langlais. "The author industry: elements of a critical theory of music ownership." Communication & Langages vol. 184, no. 2 (2015): 79–99.

11 Jean-Yves Leloup. Digital Magma: From the Utopia of Rave Parties to the iPod Generation (Paris: Scali, 2006).

12 "Content ID & Fair Use." *YouTube Help* [online]. April 22, 2010.

13 Thabet Alfishawi. "Improving Content ID." *YouTube Blog* [online]. October 3, 2012.

14 Michel Foucault. *The Order of Discourse* (Paris: Gallimard, 1971).

8 Experience as Traffic (2016–18)

1 Cécile Méadel. *Quantifier le public: histoire des mesures d'audience de la radio et de la télévision* (Paris: Economica, 2010).

2 Fabian Muniesa, Yuval Millo, and Michel Callon. "An Introduction to Market Devices," *The Sociological Review* [online], vol. 55, no. 2 (2007): 1–12.

3 Karl Polanyi. *La Subsistance de l'homme: La place de l'économie dans l'histoire et la société* (Paris: Flammarion, 2011).

4 Julie Bouchard, Étienne Candel, Hélène Cardy, and Gustavo Gomez-Mejia. *La médiatisation de l'évaluation/Evaluation in the Media* (Berne: Peter Lang AG, 2015).

5 These are tools for monitoring video viewing statistics in the spaces reserved for registered users.

6 Muniesa et al, "An Introduction to Market Devices."

7 The names and classifications of these formats are constantly changing, but the possible locations remain more or less the same.

8 *Video-related recommendations using link structure* [online]. US8145679B1, March 27, 2012.

9 Méadel, *Quantifier le public*

10 Impact Metrics. *YouTube Creator Academy* [online]. 2016.

11 Cécile Méadel. *Quantifier le public*, 42.

12 MATYSZCZYK, Chris. "Rebecca Black passes Bieber as YouTube's most hated video". *CNET* [online]. 29 mars 2011.

13 Yves Jeanneret and Valérie Patrin-Leclère. "Loft story 1 ou la critique prise au piège de l'audience,". *Hermès, La Revue* no. 3 (2003): 143–54.

14 "YouTube strips Lady Gaga of 156 million views in new scandal." *The Daily Dot* [online]. January 26, 2013.

15 Dan Ackerman Greenberg. "The Secret Strategies Behind Many 'Viral' Videos." *TechCrunch* [online]. November 22, 2007.

16 "YouTube excludes paid-ad views from its music charts and 24-hour records." *Musically.com*. September 13, 2019, p. 10.

17 "Keeping YouTube Views Authentic." *Google Online Security Blog* [online]. February 4, 2014.

18 *YouTube Creator Services Directory* [online]. [n.d.].

19 For application programming interface: "A set of standard routines that facilitate the development of applications or the manipulation of operations on a platform. An API consists of the technical infrastructure that allows access—the interface itself, the servers and authentication protocols for accessing the data—and the documentation, i.e., the set of texts that explain how the data are structured and how to access them." Goyet, *De briques et de blocs.*

20 Appadurai, "Introduction: commodities and the politics of value."

21 Susan Wojcicki. "Making ads more interesting." *Google Official Blog* [online]. March 11, 2009.

22 Karl Marx. *Le Capital I* (Montreuil: Le temps des cerises, 2009).

23 Theodor W. Adorno. "Sur Marx et les concepts de base de la théorie sociologique," in *Web revue des industries culturelles* [online]. June 1, 2018.

24 Jonathan. Martineau. *L'ère du temps: modernité capitaliste et aliénation temporelle* (Montreal: Lux éditeur, 2017).

25 Walter Benjamin. "L'œuvre d'art à l'ère de la reproductibilité technique" (1935, 1st edn), *Oeuvres. Tome III* (Paris: Gallimard, 2000).

26 Theodor W. Adorno. *Introduction à la sociologie de la musique* (Geneva: Contrechamps Éditions. 1994).

27 Jonathan Crary. *Techniques de l'observateur: vision et modernité au XIXe siècle* (Bellevaux: Éditions Dehors, 2016), 211.

28 Ibid., 227

29 Martin Kaltenecker. *L'oreille divisée: les discours sur l'écoute musicale aux XVIIIe et XIXe siècles* (Paris: Editions MF, 2010).

30 Crary, *Techniques de l'observateur.*

31 Georg Simmel. *Le cadre et autres essais* (Paris: Gallimard, 2003).

32 *YouTube Music Charts* [online]. [n.d.]. This text no longer appears on this page as of the article's revision date.

33 Composition and recording correspond to the two distinct statuses of "musical work" as established by law and by the practices of the collecting societies (see: Eligible Content in Content ID—YouTube Help [online]. [n.d.]). YouTube entered into its first agreements with a large number of economic rights management societies in 2012. Elizabeth Moody. "Sing it! YouTube opens the door for more songwriters, publishers and content creators." YouTube Blog [online]. June 5, 2012.

34 Bernhard Rieder, Ariadna Matamoros-Fernández, and Òscar Coromina. "From ranking algorithms to 'ranking cultures' Investigating the modulation of visibility in YouTube search results." *Convergence* vol. 24, no. 1 (2018): 50–68.

35 Zeynep Tufekci. "YouTube, the great radicalizer." *The New York Times.* March 10, 2018.

36 Kieran Press-Reynolds. "How TikTok Is Taking the Tunes out of Pop." *HighSnobiety* [online]. March 12, 2020.

Conclusion

1 Maria Eriksson, Rasmus Fleischer, Anna Johansson, Pelle Snickars and Patrick Vonderau. *Spotify Teardown: Inside the Black Box of Streaming Music* (Cambridge, MA: MIT Press, 2019).

2 Aaron Fernandez. "The Playlist Professionals At Apple, Spotify, And Google." *Buzzfeed.* July 13, 2016.

Bibliography

Adorno, Theodor W. *Introduction to the Sociology of Music*. Geneva: Contrechamps Éditions, 1994.

Appadurai, Arjun, ed. *The Social Life of Things*, 3–63. Cambridge: Cambridge University Press, 1986.

Benjamin, Walter. *Works. Tome III*. Paris: Gallimard, 2000.

Bennet, Andy, Barry Shank, and Jason Toynbee, eds, *The Popular Music Studies Reader*. London: Routledge, 2006.

Bennett, H. Stith, and Howard Saul Becker. *On Becoming a Rock Musician*. New York: Columbia University Press, 2017.

Berthelot-Guiet, Karine. "Extending the domain of conversation: brand discourse and publicity." *Communication & Langages* [online] vol. 169, no. 3 (2011): 77–86.

Beuscart, Jean Samuel. *The Construction of the Online Music Market: The Economic and Legal Insertion of Music Broadcasting Innovations in France*. Cachan: ENS Cachan, 2006.

Beuscart, Jean-Samuel. "Online Sociability, Virtual Notoriety and Artistic Career: The Uses of MySpace by Self-Produced Musicians." *Réseaux*, vol. 152, no. 6 (2008): 139.

Beuscart, Jean-Samuel. COAVOUX Samuel, MAILLARD Sisley, "Les algorithmes de recommandation musicale et l'autonomie de l'auditeur. Analyse des écoutes d'un panel d'utilisateurs de streaming", *Réseaux*, 2019/1 (n° 213), p. 17–47. DOI : 10.3917/res.213.0017. URL : https://www.cairn.info/revue-reseaux-2019-1-page-17.htm.

Blouin, Patrice. "On the art of Spike Jonze's video clip." *Cahiers du Cinema* vol. 14, no. 651 (2009)

Bonnet, François J. *Les mots et les sons: un archipel sonore*. Paris: Éditions de l'éclat, 2012.

Bouchard, Julie, Étienne Candel, Hélène Cardy, and Gustavo Gomez-Mejia. *La médiatisation de l'évaluation/Evaluation in the Media*. Berne: Peter Lang AG. 2015.

Bouquillion, Philippe, Bernard Miège, and Pierre Moeglin. "Content industries and communication industries: Contribution to a deconstruction of the notion of creativity." *Les Enjeux de l'Information et de la Communication* no. 16 (2018): 17–26.

Bourgatte, Michaël. "The mashup and audiovisual transtextuality on the Internet." *Communication & Langages* no. 4 (2019): 97–114.

Bullich, Vincent. "From covers to original compositions: The evolution of communicative action norms in American popular music." *Volume!* vol. 7, no. 2 (2010): 15–29.

Bullich, Vincent. "Perspectives critiques sur la propriété artistique." *Les Enjeux de l'Information et de la Communication.* no. 14/3A (2013): 81–97.

Bullich, Vincent. "Regulating amateur practices and supporting professionalization: YouTube's strategy in the race for exclusive content." *Les Enjeux de l'Information et de la Communication.* no. 16 (2015): 27–42.

Burgess, Jean, Joshua Green, and Henry Jenkins. *YouTube: Online Video and Participatory Culture.* Oxford: Wiley, 2013.

Burkart, Patrick, and Tom McCourt. "Infrastructure for the Celestial Jukebox." *Popular Music* vol. 23, no. 3 (2004): 349–62.

Cardon, Dominique, and Antonio A. Casilli *What is Digital Labor?* Bry-sur-Marne: INA, 2015.

Chabaud, Matthieu. *Music in the Picture: A Practical Guide to Using Music for Audiovisual Formats.* Paris: IRMA, 2017.

Chaney, David. "The department store as a cultural form." *Networks* vol. 14, no. 80 (1996): 81–96.

Chartier, Roger. *L'ordre des livres: lecteurs, auteurs, bibliothèques en Europe entre XIVe et XVIIIe siècle.* Aix-en-Provence: Alinea, 1992.

Chion, Michel. *L'audio-vision: son et image au cinéma.* Paris: Armand Colin, 2014.

Collins, Steve, and Sherman Young. *Beyond 2.0: The Future of Music.* Bristol, CT: Equinox Publishing, 2014.

Covington, P., Adams, J., & Sargin, E. (2016, September). Deep neural networks for youtube recommendations. In Proceedings of the 10th ACM conference on recommender systems (pp. 191–198).

Crary, Jonathan. *Techniques of the Observer: Vision and Modernity in the Nineteenth Century.* Bellevaux: Éditions Dehors, 2016

Davallon, Jean, ed., *The Economics of Writing on the Web*, 165–201. Cachan: Hermès Science Publications-Lavoisier, 2012.

De Montety, Caroline. "Brand magazines: between 'semiotic management' and the kitchen of meaning." *Communication & Langages* (2005): 35–48.

Dolan, Emily I. "'. . This little ukulele tells the truth': Indie pop and kitsch authenticity." *Popular Music* vol. 29, no. 3 (2010): 457–69.

Drotner, Kirsten, Hans Siggaard Jensen, and Kim Schrøder, eds, Informal Learning and Digital Media. Newcastle, UK: Cambridge Scholars, 2008.

Emigh, Jacqueline. "New Flash Player Rises in the Web-Video Market", *Computer* vol. 39, no. 2 (2006): 14–16.

Eriksson, Maria, Rasmus Fleischer, Anna Johansson, Pelle Snickars and Patrick Vonderau. *Spotify Teardown: Inside the Black Box of Streaming Music.* Cambridge, MA: MIT Press, 2019.

Feld, S. A. "Sweet Lullaby for World Music." Public Culture vol. 12, no. 1 (2000): 145–71.

Fisher, Mark. *Ghosts of My Life: Writings on Depression, Hauntology and Lost Futures.* Alresford: John Hunt Publishing, 2014.

Fisher, Mark. *K-Punk: The Collected and Unpublished Writings of Mark Fisher (2004–2016).* London: Repeater, 2018.

Foucault, Michel. *The Order of Discourse.* Paris: Gallimard, 1971.

Gilbert, Jeremy and Pearson, Ewan. *Discographies: Dance Music, Culture and the Politics of Sound.* London: Psychology Press, 1999.

Gillespie, Tarleton. "Governance Of and By Platforms," in *The Sage Handbook of Social Media,* edited by Jean Burgess, Alice Marwick, and Thomas Poell. 1st edn. Thousand Oaks, CA: SAGE inc, 2017.

Goehr, Lydia. *The Imaginary Museum of Musical Works.* Paris: La Rue Musicale, 2018.

Goldstein, Paul. *Copyright's Highway: From Gutenberg to the Celestial Jukebox.* Stanford, CA: Stanford Law and Politics, 2003.

Goldstone, Andrew. "MP3 Blogs: A Silver Bullet for the Music Industry or a Smoking Gun for Copyright Infringement?" SSRN Electronic Journal (2006).

Gomez-Mejia, Gustavo. "What is the Cloud? The status of media in the face of cloud computing regimes." *Communication & Langages* vol. 182, no. 4 (2014): 77–93.

Goyet, Samuel. "Of bricks and blocks. The editorial function of web APIs: between combinatorial science and text industry." PhD thesis. Paris: Celsa Paris-Sorbonne, November 22, 2017.

Greif, Mark. *Against Everything: Essays.* New York: Pantheon Books, 2016.

Grignon, Thomas. "Communicative expertise through the prism of its instruments. L'exemple de Google Analytics." Les Cahiers du RESIPROC no. 3 (2015): 23–47.

Grignon, Thomas. "Quand Google fait école. Une prétention pédagogique en question." *Communication & Langages* [online] vol. 188, no. 2 (2016): 123–39.

Guibert, Gérôme. "Indie-pop. Analyse d'un courant musical." Master's thesis in sociology. Nantes: University of Nantes, 1996.

Heald, Paul J. "How Notice-and-Takedown Regimes Create Markets for Music on YouTube: An Empirical Study." *SSRN Electronic Journal* 2014.

Hebdige, Dick. *Subculture: A Sense of Style.* Paris: La Découverte, 2008.

Heins, Marjorie. "The brave new world of social media censorship." *Harv. L. Rev.* vol. 127 (2013).

Hesmondhalgh, David. "Post-Punk's attempt to democratize the music industry: the success and failure of Rough Trade." *Popular Music* vol. 16, no. 3 (1997): 255.

Heuguet, Guillaume. "New 'crossroads' in the mediatization of musical success: About the song 'Alaska' by Maggie Rogers." *Volume!* vol. 15, no. 2 (2018): 97–117.

Hillrichs, Rainer. "Poetics of Early YouTube: Production, Performance, Success." PhD dissertation, Faculty of Philosophy. Universitäts-und Landesbibliothek Bonn: Universitäts-und Landesbibliothek Bonn, 2005.

Hochschild, Arlie Russell, Salomé Fournet-Fayas, and Cécile Thomé. *The Price of Feelings: At the Heart of Emotional Labor.* Paris: La Découverte, 2017.

James, Robin. "Songs of myself." Audimat no. 12 (2019).

Jeanneret, Yves. *Critique of Triviality: The Mediations of Communication, A Stake in Power.* Paris: Éditions Non standard, 2014.

Jeanneret, Yves, and Valérie Patrin-Leclère. "Loft story 1 ou la critique prise au piège de l'audience." *Hermès, La Revue* no. 3 (2003): 143–54.

Kaltenecker, Martin. *L'oreille divisée: les discours sur l'écoute musicale aux XVIIIe et XIXe siècles.* Paris: Editions MF, 2010.

Kim, Jin. "The institutionalization of YouTube: From user-generated content to professionally generated content." *Media, Culture & Society* vol. 34, no. 1 (2012): 53–67.

Labelle, Sarah. "La ville inscrite dans 'la société de l'information': formes d'investissement d'un objet symbolique." PhD thesis in Information and Communication Sciences. Paris: Celsa–Paris IV Sorbonne, 2007.

Lacy, Sarah. *The Stories of Facebook, YouTube and MySpace: The People, the Hype and the Deals behind the Giants of Web 2.0.* [s.l.]: Crimson Publishing, 2009.

Langlais, Pierre-Carl. "The author industry: elements of a critical theory of music ownership." *Communication & Langages* vol. 184, no. 2 (2015): 79–99.

Leloup, Jean-Yves. *Digital Magma: From the Utopia of Rave Parties to the iPod Generation.* Paris: Scali, 2006.

Maisonneuve, Sophie. *L'invention du disque: 1877–1949; genèse de l'usage des médias musicaux contemporains.* Paris: Éd. des Archives Contemporaines, 2009.

Majean, Romane. *YouTube: Enjeux de visibilité de la minorité queer afro-américaine à travers les clips de hip-hop Les cas de Mykki Blanco, Cakes Da Killa et Big Freedia. Mémoire de maîtrise.* Paris: Celsa Paris Sorbonne, 2017.

Marshall, Lee. "For and against the record industry: an introduction to bootleg collectors and tape traders." *Popular Music* vol. 22, no. 1 (2003).

Martineau, Jonathan, and Colette St-Hilaire. *The Time Age: Capitalist Modernity and Temporal Alienation.* Montreal: Lux éditeur, 2017.

Marx, Karl. *Capital I.* Montreuil: Le temps des cerises, 2009.

McIntosh, Heather. "Vevo and the Business of Online Music Video Distribution." Popular Music and Society vol. 39, no. 5 (2016): 487–500.

McRobbie, Angela. *Be Creative: Making a Living in the New Culture Industries.* Hoboken, NJ: Wiley, 2018.

Méadel, Cécile. *Quantifying the Audience: A History of Audience Measurement in Radio and Television.* Paris: Economica, 2010.

Menger, Pierre-Michel. *Profession artiste: extension du domaine de la création.* Paris: Textuel, 2005.

Morin, Edgar. *L'esprit du temps.* Paris: Grasset, 1962.

Mulligan, Mark. Awakening: The Music Industry in the Digital Age. [s. l.]: MIDiA Research, 2015.

Muniesa, Fabian, Yuval Millo, and Michel Callon. "An Introduction to Market Devices." The Sociological Review vol. 55, no. 2 (2007): suppl, pp. 1–12.

O'Donnell, Patrick, and Steven McClung. "MP3 Music Blogs: Their Efficacy in Selling Music and Marketing Bands." Atlantic Journal of Communication vol. 16, no. 2 (2008): 71–87.

Polanyi, Karl. *The Subsistence of Man: The Place of Economics in History and Society.* Paris: Flammarion, 2011.

Rieder, Bernhard, Ariadna Matamoros-Fernández, and Òscar Coromina. "From ranking algorithms to 'ranking cultures': Investigating the modulation of visibility in YouTube search results." *Convergence* vol. 24, no. 1 (2018): 50–68.

San Filippo, Maria. "A Cinema Of Recession: Micro-budgeting, microdrama, and the 'mumblecore' movement." Cineaction no. 85 (2011): 2–8.

Scott, Derek B. *Sounds of the Metropolis.* New York: Oxford University Press, 2008.

Seidler, David. "The Right to Copyright? Mp3 Blogs and the Rise of the Online Taste-Makers." SSRN Electronic Journal (2010).

Seyfert, Robert, and Jonathan Roberge, eds, *Algorithmic Cultures: Essays on Meaning, Performance and New Technologies* (1st edn). London and New York: Routledge, 2016.

Shklovski, Irina, and D. Boyd. *Music as Cultural Glue: Supporting Bands and Fans on MySpace.* Unpublished Tech Report. 2006.

Simmel, Georg. *The Frame and Other Essays.* Paris: Gallimard, 2003.

Smythe, Dallas W. *On the Audience Commodity and Its Work,* 230–56. Media and cultural studies: Keywords. 1981.

Supiot, Alain. *La gouvernance par les nombres: cours au Collège de France, 2012–2014.* Paris: Fayard, 2015.

Szendy, Peter. Tubes: *Philosophy in the Jukebox.* Paris: Éditions de Minuit, 2008.

Thornton, Sarah. Club *Cultures: Music, Media, and Subcultural Capital.* Hanover, NH: University Press of New England, 1996.

Toynbee, Jason. *Making Popular Music: Musicians, Creativity and Institutions*. London: Arnold, 2000.

UNESCO. *Cultural Industries: A Challenge for the Future of Culture*, 21–36. Paris: Unesco, 1982.

Vaidhyanathan, Siva. *Copyrights and Copywrongs: The Rise of Intellectual Property and How It Threatens Creativity*. New York: New York University Press, 2003.

Vandiedonck, David. *What Makes the Classical Record Roll? Logiques éditoriales et place des interprètes*. Villeneuve d'Ascq: Presses universitaires du Septentrion, 1999.

Vonderau, Patrick, and Pelle Snickars, eds, *The YouTube Reader*, 154–66. Stockholm: National Library of Sweden, 2009.

Wade Morris, Jeremy. *Selling Digital Music: Formatting Culture*. Berkeley, CA: University of California Press, 2015.

Wade Morris, Jeremy, and Evan Elkins. "There's a History for That: Apps and Mundane Software as Commodity." *The Fibreculture Journal* no. 25 (2015): 63–88.

Washburne, Christopher J., and Maiken Derno, eds, *Bad Music: The Music We Love to Hate*. London: Routledge, 2013.

Watson, Allan, and Jenna Ward. "Creating the right 'vibe': Emotional labour and musical performance in the recording studio." *Environment and Planning A* vol. 45, no. 12 (2013): 2904–18.

Wiener, Norbert. *Cybernetics and Society: The Human Use of Human Beings*. Paris: Points, 2014.

Williams, Raymond, and Ederyn Williams. *Television: Technology and Cultural Form*. London and New York: Routledge, 2003.

Index